The Aut

Bu

Y.B.I.

Young Boy's Inc.

As told to Raymond L. Canty

P.O. Box 32579
Detroit, MI 48232-0579

By Raymond L. Canty, Milton Jones, and Julius Jus

Y.B.I (Young Boy's Inc.)
The autobiography of Butch Jones
An H. Publication Book/July 1996

Book design by Raymond L. Canty, Milton Jones, and Julius Justice

 ISBN 1-889557-00-5

Contents

Chapter 1

Makin' Bones

I was fourteen years old when I was brought into the dope game. My brother-in-law, Dr. Bombay, was the guy who brought me in. Although he wasn't a real doctor in the sense of the word, he was a master operator. He could take a bag of heroin, mix it, flip it and pile up dollars equal to any medical doctor during his day.

I first started workin' for my brother-in-law after school, and right away, I became fascinated with the whole scene. Back then Dr. Bombay used to sell what was known as penny caps. Penny Caps was heroin that was measured in small quantities and then sold for a dollar each.

My initial job was security. I would go to the door with my pistol and make sure everythang remained in order. I would observe the transaction, and after it went smoothly I would wait on the next one. I'd always hoped somebody would try somethin', just anythang, and one day somebody would.

You gotta' realize, I grew up in the 70's when movies like Superfly, The Mack, and Hell Up In Harlem dominated the big screen. So as far as I was concerned, this was my big chance to be what I saw, and I wasn't about to blow it.

Back in those days the operation would gross about eight or nine hundred dollars a day, and my take would be two hundred dollars a week.

When I was fourteen, two hundred dollars went a long way. There was no such thing as hundred dollar gym shoes, a hundred and fifty dollar blue jeans, or seventy five dollar shirts. Two hundred dollars then is what a thousand dollars is today. You could buy a nice pair of Converse All Stars for ten dollars, a pair of swedish knit pants for twenty and a Knik Knik or Roland shirt for twelve dollars. And if you were into hard shoes, you could get a nice pair of quality shoes for fifty dollars. When I say nice, I mean shoes that today would cost you at least three hundred dollars. And blue jeans were no more than ten dollars, period.

The one thang I always did when I got paid was give my mother some of my money. That always made me feel like I was bringin' somethin' to the household. And in fact, I was.

My mother never really questioned me about where

the money came from because I was always doing odd jobs around the neighborhood so she just assumed that's where I got it.

From the day I started workin' for my brother-in-law, it didn't take much proddin' to convince me that pushin' drugs was the thing for me. When I saw how easy money could be made, and how the same people would come back again and again, man I was hooked.

After some months of workin' for Dr. Bombay, I met this guy named Black Joe. I started sellin' heroin for him in 1971. By this time selling dope had become a 24 hour a day occupation for me. When I met Joe things really began to escalate. He showed me thangs on a much higher level.

It was at this point that I moved up from sellin' penny caps and started sellin' quarters, half ounces, ounces or whatever anybody wanted, because Joe was gettin' kilo's.

In the dope game you can really start making a lot of money fast. That's why a lot of people get caught up in it. You can be sittin' around tryna' live a normal life and then you see people around you, no smarter than you makin' big bank and after awhile you're like fuck it. I'll just get me a couple thousand then I'm out.

But of course it's never just a couple thousand. 'Cause once you get that first thousand then you want another and another and another. It's just like the people you sellin' to. They hooked on the drug and you're hooked on the money.

It got so good for me, that while my friends were catchin' buses to school, I was catchin' cabs. While everybody else would get into a fight, and at the worse, stab somebody, I was shootin' niggas at the drop of a dime.

So you see, I became a menace at an early age. I had a reputation that couldn't be touched.

I killed my first person when I was fifteen. It was cold blooded murder. And basically, after the first time I did it, killin' became second nature to me. What I mean by second nature, is that, I could easily kill somebody and not lose a second of sleep. That's when you know you a real O.G.

If you kill somebody and you tossin' an' turnin' all night, then you know you ain't got the stomach for murder.

In the streets they call what I was doing makin' my bones. Making your bones basically means that you have heart and don't mind provin' it if somebody get's in your way.

The first person I ever killed was this punk from across Linwood name Stick-Up Mike. He was known for robbin' dope houses and then killing everybody in the house. He didn't believe in leaving any livin' evidence when he did his dirt, so if he robbed your house somebody would soon be callin' your momma to tell her you was dead.

Anyway, one day, me, Al Baby, Uncle Herman, Bolmolt, Rickey Terrell, and David Easly were all sittin' in the house on Duane takin' care of our business when all of a sudden we heard a knock at the door. So Al Baby went to the door to see who it was. After slightly opening the door and peekin' out, he quickly closed it and stated that some strange chick was at the door.

So, I asked Uncle Herman to check it out, 'cause me and Uncle Herman knew every customer. Uncle Herman went to the door looked out then turned and said that some lady he didn't know was out there and there was this guy who was kinda' standing behind her who looked like Stick-up Mike.

So, I went to the door and eased it open just enough to peek out.

Damn, I thought. I couldn't believe it. It was Stick Up Mike. The mothafucka' known for going to drug houses and killin' everybody in it.

All a sudden, I got so nervous I could hardly think. I just started shakin', 'cause this guy had obviously come to kill us and like any human with common sense I got scared. For a quick second the face of death slapped me dead in the face but that same slap also woke me up.

I was scared, but I wasn't about to just up and let somebody kill me, especially in no dope house. That would be like dying of cirrhosis of the liver, you know. You might be doing wrong but you still wanna" die wit' some sense of dignity, so a dope house was the last place I wanted to get killed. Niggas who get caught with their pants down die in dope houses, so quite naturally, that's the last place I wanted to be found dead.

Anyway, we had this 12 gauge shotgun that we had bought from the pawnshop sittin' in the corner. So I picked it up and I crept up to the door and again peeked out, 'cause I didn't even want Mike to know I was in the house, just in case somethin' went wrong. That's how scared I was.

So, I cracked open the door and before anybody knew what was happenin', I blew the mothafucka' about five feet back in the air. I caught everybody off guard.

For a few seconds everybody was lookin' at each other and then all at once everybody started sayin', "Damn, Butch, you done killed Stick-Up Mike. Damn! What you gone do na'?"

I was like, "Fuck that nigga'. He was gone do us. So fuck 'em. I ain't tryna' go out like that."

That was my first murder and after that day, I never gave killin' a second thought.

After word got around about what I'd done, I didn't have no more trouble outta' nobody in that neighborhood. Especially from the people on the other side of Linwood where Stick-Up Mike was from.

Because of the shooting, Joe moved his hustle over to Tuxedo and when it cooled down a bit I reopened the spot where the shootin' had taken' place. We didn't lose any of our clientele when Joe moved, because we had some good stuff. Joe didn't have a problem with it cause wit' the type of shit we had (Mexican Mud which Joe bought directly from Mexico) you could just about open a spot anywhere and get paid. You gotta' realize, back then it was nothin' like it is now. You didn't have people on every other block sellin' drugs, so if you opened a spot it was as good as gold.

My life became real cool when I got my own spot, I was on top of the world.

Another thing I learned during this time was how to gamble. And with all the money I was makin', it wasn't long before I was gamblin' with the big fellas.

There was this one place called the Chess and Cue and I use to go down there a lot. Bob Ridgeway, who was a barber by day and a pimp by night owned the joint. Bob like a lot of older players took a likin' to me and let me hang out wit' the big boys. Back then, I was the youngest guy allowed in the joint. It was like the top of the line after-hours place, and all the big time hustlers hung out there.

Honky Tonk Bud, hung out there. Race Car Red, Milwaukee Jack, Hog Mog George, you know people like that. Memphis Slim, Texas Slim, Fast Eddie and my main man Tall Paul. Man, soon as I would walk through the door the first person you would hear was Tall Paul sayin', "What they hit fo'? Boy throw yo' shot up." Man, that was the life. And talk about cheatin', shit that's all I use to do 'cause that was the best way to keep the cheat off you.

I remember how whenever I would see Tall Paul I would throw him thirty or forty dollars for luck. It wasn't because he needed the money, it was more a less just a good luck type of thang. Sometimes it worked and sometimes it didn't.

Anyway, Tall Paul had this pretty, powdered blue two door Cadillac Eldorado and he used to let me take it to get washed at the car wash up on Dexter and Elmhurst. After I would get the car washed, I would drive down Dexter, just crusin' with the music blastin'.

Man, you couldn't tell me nothin'. I would have the top down, and all you could hear blastin' was the song "I'll take you there" by the Staple Singers.

I never took the car back on time, but Tall Paul didn't mind, he wasn't pressed like that. After I would get tired of driving the car up and down Dexter I'd ride over to Highland Park and hang out.

Highland Park is a small city that cut's right through Detroit, but those girls were a little different from the girls in my neighborhood, they had a little mo' class. See, my neighborhood was basically the ghetto, so a lot of the girls didn't really want nothin' outta' life. No more than welfare. You know for a while that was the thang. Get you a coupla' kids and get on welfare. Well, I wanted more outta' life than that. So, I would go to Highland Park and hang out with the girls there.

Now mind you this was still only 1971 and I was only fifteen. But that didn't stop me. As I think about it, it was also the year I met my wife, Portia, who was also fifteen at the time. I really liked hangin' out with Portia and her girls because they were all real pretty. She hung out with Kathy, Faye, Lisa, Darcell, and Vera. All real pretty. But the one girl that stood out to me was

Portia. She was as cute as a button, and as innocent as could be. She didn't know nothin' about the streets.

But of course as Young Boy's Inc. would later become notorious all that would later change.

Anyway, by this time, I had a Ph. D. in the streets. There wasn't nothin' anybody could tell me that I didn't know. Man, I would break in houses, steal cars, steal car batteries; man I was just bad. I would steal aluminum doors, Michelin tires just anything you could think of. Peoples artificial grass. I remember the time that my neighbors, Linda and Brenda, had gotten some new sod, so I went around the corner to this boy John Brown's house and asked his father if he wanted to buy some grass and he said sure. So I waited until three in the mornin' and I stole Linda and Brenda's grass as well as the lawn chairs off their porch and sold it all to John Brown's father. They never knew it was me who'd stole their sod and lawn chairs.

Sometimes when I got bored with being in Highland Park, I would bring Portia and her girls over to our side of town. Compared ta' Highland Park, Dexter was like a whole new world to them. See, nobody sold dope or did the shit we did in Highland Park. It was like a hick town compared to Detroit.

Money was plentiful too. Back then, we would cut the heroin with lactose. We would use one quarter heroin and two quarter lactose. This is what was called a two. The profit margin was, if you invested a thousand, then you would get three thousand back. That was a hellava profit margin.

By this time, I had also gotten a great reputation, because if a person sellin' the drug didn't have any or ran out, he could always get some from Joe, because Joe always had it, but what this meant was that if they had to get it from Joe they actually had to get it from me, because I was the go to man.

Dexter was cookin' back then. You had your prostitutes, your sissies, your pimps, your hustlers and I knew 'em all. Me and all the other pushers all hung out together. We would shoot pool, shoot dice, play cards, or whatever else we could that included gambling.

It was also about this time that my life escalated to yet another level. That of takin' assignments. An assignment could include any number of different jobs and eventually I would cover a wide range.

My first assignment was arson. My job was to burn down a coupla' supermarkets. I didn't know whose supermarkets they were, what the deal behind the acts were, and frankly I didn't give a fuck. I got paid five hundred dollars a piece for them and that's all I needed to know. Burning up shit was pretty easy, all I would do is make up some Molotov cocktails, hire a driver, pull up in front of the store and blast the mothafucka'. Easy money.

After my first few assignments, I got my first, or at least what I call my first real assignment: murder.

What happened was this guy who use to hang out at the club gamblin' all the time had gotten himself killed after being caught cheatin' in cards. He was a professional cheat. He could do anythang with a deck of cards, unfortunately, it's always somebody out there with an eye quicker than yours, and that's when yo' life can very well end. And that's what happened ta' blood.

Anyway, one of the guys went to prison over the murder but the other one got away. Eventually however the one that got away ended up pissin' off some people and because of it, became my first murder assignment. I was paid two thousand dollars to hunt him down. I was warned by the guy who paid me, that my target was a real hard person to get, so be very careful 'cause he was suppose to be a tough mothafucka' and if I was caught slippin' I could forget it. He had a reputation for bein' one who didn't take no shit off nobody and the fact that he had killed a few times in cold blood kinda' attested to this fact.

After a couple days, I found out where my target lived and I began watchin' him.

From watchin' him I discovered that every mornin' around 7:00 he would step outside to take out his garbage. I couldn't believe it. Didn't he know that niggas was lookin' for him? It was at this point that he fucked up. My plan was in motion.

The night before the actual murder was to take place it became the longest night of my life. I was excited, anxious and nervous all at the same time, because this guy was supposed to be a tough guy and I just wanted to see his face when I popped him. So I was excited because of the thrill, anxious because I wanted to get it done, and nervous because I didn't want anything to go wrong.

So, that mornin', I got up at five o'clock and had my boy Sid The Kid to drop me off near the site where the assignment would take place. I then walked down the alley and jumped down into the garbage container where my target emptied his trash. When I jumped down into the dumpster rats started dashin' about the container and I got a little nervous about 'em, but I was like fuck it, I ain't got time to be concerned about no rats. I just wanted to keep all my energy concentrated on this guy. All I wanted at this point was just to see the expression on this guy's face when I did him. He was supposed to be so tough, so I was itchin' to find out just how tough he was when a 9mm was pointed at his face. I was like a little kid in a candy store and I couldn't wait to get my candy.

In view of the cause for my being in the dumpster, it seemed like hours before my target came out, but in reality it was more like a half hour. Then just like clockwork I heard him approaching. With each step came the anticipation of death. What was actually seconds seemed like minutes, until suddenly, he lifted the cover of the dumpster and there I was. I popped up like a Jack in the box. And he froze. He was in total shock. For a few seconds all he could do was stare. Stare with the look of death. He knew he was dead, there was no if's, ands, or butt's about it.

You might wonder what I mean by the look of

death, well everybody whose ever been killed probably has a different one, but the bottom line is when you know you're about to die that's the look I'm talkin' about. Anyway, all at once he just took off runnin' and I began blastin' that nigga' dead in his back. Ta dow, pow, pow. Ta dow. If that's the way he wanted it, then that's the way I was gonna' give it to 'em. It wasn't long before the gun just began clickin'. At first, I thought the gun was jammed, but I later realized it wasn't jammed at all. I had merely emptied the clip in that mothafucka'. I'd shot him in the back fifteen times.

When I reported back to the guy that had given me the assignment, he was amazed that I had done such a good job. He asked me how I had ended up shootin' my man in the back and I explained the whole thang to him.

After that, I began to get a lot of assignments and with the number of assignments came more money. First two thousand dollars, then five thousand and before you knew it, ten thousand dollars. I was rich. To me, what I was doing was no different than anybody else's job. The only difference was that my job was to kill people and I took great pride in my craft.

Man, I could sit and wait for a person for twenty-four hours. Sometimes just waitin' behind bushes. No food, no water, nothin'. I was like the man lookin' for Charlie. I was at war, only the enemy never knew I was there until it was too late. That's the way it is in the streets. Live by the sword die by the sword and it was my job to make sure you died by it.

Anytime, I would make some money I would never forget my homeboys. Baby Ray, Block, Bomolt, Uncle Herman, Rickey Terrell, David Mennifie, Walter Mennifie, Jimmie, Stony Ronie, just to name a few, all of us hung out together. They knew I sold dope, but they never knew I was takin' people out.

You know I guess I never really told anybody because although I was as raw as you could get, I knew that deep down inside that what I was doing was wrong and I never would have wanted my family and close friends to know that I was out there killin' people like that. All the pay for hire killings would later be one of the things I would kinda' later regret. But at 15 years old I was to intent on makin' my bones and I wasn't gone let nothin' get in my way of doin' that.

Out of all my friends during this time, my boy Block stood out from the pack 'cause he had a lot of heart. He was like me. When we went to parties, we would never go to a party to dance. We would go to fight. We was from Martindale and was known as the wreckin' crew. I would stand around and touch a girl's ass, knowin' she would go back and tell her boyfriend and of course she would and the fight was on.

Also back then, if you fucked a girl, everybody got some pussy. Ya' know, we would toss her up like a tossed salad. It wasn't no, "That's yo' bitch", nah it was everybody's bitch. Except for Block. He was kinda pussy shy. He would always be back at the girls house robbin' it while we was fuckin'.

Block was a true character. The way we met was kinda' funny. One day, me and my boy was out shovelin' snow and we knocked on these people's door. We asked if we could shovel their snow and they was like okay. So, we started shovelin'. We shoveled the driveway, and then the front. We did a real good job.

When we went to get our money the girl who had said okay came to the door with some play monopoly money. We was like, "Bitch, where's our money?" In the meantime, Block was standin' behind the girl laughin' an' shit. I mean here was this nigga' wit' this big ass block head laughin' and we was mad as hell. So, we was like alright then, when we catch his ass on the street we gone fuck him up. So for the time bein', we took all the snow, threw it back where we got it and stepped on it.

Just like we thought, it wasn't long before we ran into Block. He was walkin' down the street. He had some skates wit' him, so I guess he was goin' skatin'. Anyway, we was about to wreck my man, but a guy we was with, was like; "Man, that's my nigga'. That's Block. He cool as hell."

So, from that day on, me and Block became friends. You know how that shit is, you gotta' respect a nigga' wit' heart, especially if he's from your own 'hood.

After that, me and Block started rippin' off things together. The first thang I learned from Block was about goin' into supermarkets and rippin' off steaks. The way you would do it, is you would buy a fifty pound bag of dog food and pour it all out. Then later, you would sneak the bag back into another store and fill it up with steaks and other expensive meats. Then, you would staple the bag up and take it to the cashier. You might spend five dollars for the dog food but have four hundred dollars worth of steaks. It was a lot of money in that lil' scheme, so we did that a lot.

After awhile, I got to the point where I would say fuck buyin' anythang. I would go into the store, empty out the dog food in the middle of the floor, (outta' sight of course), and fill the mothafucka' up and then take it to the cashier.

Man, the shit was real good back then. For example, four of us would go into a restaurant to eat. After we ate, first, one person would get up, then another person, then before you knew it there was one person left and that person would run out the restaurant hollerin' "Rip!"

Other things we would do is go to the record store and have the lady get all the top albums out for us. The Temptations, Jackson Five, Staple Singers, and anybody else that had a hit. And after she got all the albums and handed them to us we would run outta' the store hollerin' "Rip, Rip!". Or we would go to the cleaners and tell the lady that my name was Zimmerman, so she would have to go all the way to the back of the cleaners lookin' for my name. Then, we would pop open the cash register snatch the money and run. On other days we would go to the cab stand and wait on the cab driver to get out for any reason and when he did, we would snatch his box and run down the street hollerin' "Rip"!

Man, all that stuff was fun. The first time we ever got caught stealin'was as a result of something we'd stole in school. I had peeped this teacher named Mrs. Brown stashin' her money in her purse and then put it in the closet. Well, the way we handled that was that my boy got Mrs. Brown to go out into the hall by actin' like he needed some help after school. Damn, I laugh everytime I think about that incident. Anyway, while she was out there, I crept over to the closet and ripped off her money. We then waited until lunch time and instead of goin' ta' lunch and comin' back, we went to Hudson's down-town and bought us some James Bond attaché cases.

When I got home though, Mrs. Brown was waitin' for me at my house. I was like, "Damn, how did she know it was us?" Of course she knew, because we were the only ones who didn't come back from lunch, not to mention the fact that I came home with all kinds of money in my pockets. Man, my parents beat my ass for that shit. That was the first time we ever got caught doing anything. But I was like fuck it. We went back up to the school and knocked out all of Mrs. Brown's car windows. We didn't give a fuck, everythang to us back then was fun and games.

Now I know you're probably thinkin' wasn't I just talkin' about killin' people only a few pages back and now I'm talkin' 'bout school an' shit, but that's how it was with me. School, killin', drugs, stealin' I was doing it all. And just like the killins' I don't know what I was thinkin' when we did that shit to Mrs. Brown. The only thing she ever tried to do for us was help, but we were just to bent on hell and destruction. Mrs. Brown really was a good person. But at the time we didn't give a fuck.

Also right about this time, I started collectin' guns. Whenever I would go over ta' Joe's, people would bring guns over. You could get a gun for fifty dollars. So I had about nineteen or twenty pistols.

Anyway, one day we were in our drug spot on Martindale and this cop named Rudy Davis came in and busted us. While he was there, he looked at me and said, "You that nigga' that's been sellin' all the dope around here ain't you?" I was like, "Man, I don't know what you talkin' about." Then, outta' nowhere he just slapped me in the face. Bam! and said, "Nigga, you full of shit, me and my partner been watchin' you for days sell dope."

Meantime, Dart Bart who was with me put his head down toward the floor, because he didn't want Rudy Davis to walk over to him and slap the shit outta' him. So while Dart was still lookin' down and I was standin' there wonderin' what this fool was gonna do next, Rudy rounded up all our guns and dope and just walked out the door like the shit belonged to him.

After about the third or fourth time Rudy busted us I was like, "Hey fuck this shit. Everytime you come in here all you do is take our shit. You ain't no better than none of us. You ain't tryna' bust us, you just tryna' keep our shit. You pimpin' us." Rudy looked at me and pulled out his pistol and stuck it up to my face. "Nigga," he said, "If you ever in yo' life say anythang to anybody about this shit or ever say anythang to me again about this shit, I'll kill yo' mothafuckin' ass. Do you understand me?"

At that point, I knew what it meant to stare death directly in the face, because I knew he wasn't bullshittin'. After that, whenever I would see or even hear that Rudy Davis was ridin' around the hood, I would close down. Because that was one guy that did intimidate me. Here was this guy that had the law behind him, a gun, and was also crazy as hell, so hell yeah that fool scared me.

Eventually, there was an investigation in the 10th precinct because as it turned out, Rudy Davis wasn't the only police officer going around rippin' off people and keepin' everythang. Everybody over there was doing it. It was a real big scandal. It was in all the papers and on t.v. And that's when Rudy Davis got busted.

Gettin' rid of him was the best thang that the police department could have ever done. Man did they do me a big favor.

Chapter 2

Jail

By 1973 I was spending a lot of my time with this guy named Parhoo. Me and Parhoo had become friends basically just from growin' up in the neighborhood. Life hadn't got much different by seventy-three. The one main difference though, was now I was back on Martindale sellin' weight from over my mommas house instead of some other location. Of course I was doing this on a real quiet tip, because my momma and daddy didn't want the stuff in they house. So instead of everybody just poppin' up like they normally would, you had to call first.

Anyway, one day Parhoo came over to the crib and asked me if I had a gun. So knowin' somethin' was up, I sent Portia downstairs 'cause at that time I didn't like her to be involved in any of my business. So after she left, I told Parhoo, "Of course I had a gun. Why?" And he was like "'Cause Leroy's sister Jackie just got robbed over in Highland Park." So, I asked him if the people that did it knew me and he said, "No." So, I said, "Cool." So, me and Parhoo went and scooped up my boy Leroy who was also a straight up dog, and Jackie of course so she could show us where to go and we headed over to the location where the robbery had taken place.

The place where the robbery had taken place was up over one of those storefronts but the store over which the people lived was closed, so, Jackie knocked on the door leading to the upstairs and after a few minutes, a lady, not peepin' to see we was with Jackie just opened the door.That's when we busted in and stepped up in the joint.

After we got in, the only people we saw was this guy, the lady, and her baby. So while keepin' my eyes on the guy I began casin' the joint and checkin' the closets ta' make sure nobody else was in the apartment while Leroy began to check the other rooms.

After I finished lookin' in the closets, the guy, who was tall, well built and in his mid twenties stood up. So I told him to sit down 'cause Jackie had already indicated to us he wasn't the guy we was lookin' for. So I told him to just sit down and relax 'cause we didn't come for him. I think my man thought we was playin' or somethin', 'cause he kept gettin' up and I kept havin' to tell him to sit down.

Eventually, just out of the blue this fool lunged at me with this karate move, so I shot the mothafucka. Everybody back then thought they was Bruce Lee and I guess my man was no different. Anyway I just shot him in the foot, 'cause like I said, we hadn't come for him.

You would have never known we hadn't come for him though, 'cause even after I shot him he jumped up again and tried to throw some more karate. But this time Leroy who'd come back into the room saw what the guy was tryin' ta' do and just went berserk on my man. He started stabbin' him every which way but loose. Remember, like I said, Leroy was a stone raw dog and he didn't give a fuck about nothin' or nobody.

After Leroy stabbed Bruce Lee Jr. about a hundred times the guy just slumped to the floor in a big mass of blood. At that point Leroy began pacin' the house like a mad man. "Let's kill everybody up in this bitch, he began shoutin'. Let's kill the mothafuckin' baby, that bitch and anybody else that step up in this mothafucka'."

When he said baby, I was like, "Baby! Man, you need ta' chill."

But he was intent on killin' everybody.

At that point I told Parhoo and Jackie ta' go downstairs and wait in the car. Then, I told Leroy, "Look Leroy, let me handle this. I'll do the killin'. Why don't you go and wait in the car with them and I'll do them. You owe me one anyway. So after a little fuss, he finally went on downstairs.

Now, my man who had been shot and stabbed, he

was all fucked up so I didn't really have ta' worry about him. He looked like he'd just jumped from an airplane without a parachute and had landed face down on the sidewalk. Man, his own momma wouldn't have recognized him had she walked in. Blood was oozin' out of every part of his body and the only sounds you could hear comin' from his direction, were the grunts of death.

After Leroy had disappeared downstairs I walked over to the lady, her name was Linda. I said, "Look, I'm not gonna do nothin' to you and yo' baby, but if you say anythang to anybody about what happened, I'm gonna come back for you." I really wasn't worried about her though because she didn't know me. She'd never seen me before that day so my words were basically just a formality.

When we got back to the west side we drove straight to Monterey Street. When we got there, the first person I saw was Block. I told Block how we'd just had to do this 187 and how I didn't wanna' fuck up my man, but he kept tryna' throw karate, so we had to fuck him up.

We then went over to Tuxedo, 'cause I was lookin' for Robert Jr., 'cause he was my man and we wanted to let him know we had taken care of some business for him. Robert Jr. was also Leroy's brother and of course Jackie's brother.

After we got over there, come to find out, while we were in Highland Park, Robert Jr. had robbed this guy from the hood named Pretty Boy, a petty robbery, ya' know. So, we sittin' up in the crib waitin' on Robert Jr.

and all a sudden we hear this noise. Boom! Boom! And we get outside and Robert Jr. in the car dead. Pretty Boy done killed him. I was like "Goddamn!" 'cause I had never had nobody in my crew to get murdered. So I was fucked up.

So, I rounded up everybody from my crew and headed out on my mission. I had gotten these hand grenades from my friend John Brown who had been in Vietnam, special forces.

I'd had a coupla friends who had been to Nam and had brought back some shit. My boy Wally B had brought back some shit, Jimmie had brought some shit back and of course John Brown. Plus, I made sure I rounded up my boy Clark, because he was a demolition man, not to mention the fact that he use to fight pit bulls with me. He was a raw dog.

When we got to Pretty Boy's house, there was a vacant lot right next to his house. So I lined everybody up and after makin' sure everybody was ready, I gave the signal. After about 10 minutes of shootin' up the house, I told Clark to throw the hand grenade, so he pulled the pin, threw it through the window and Boom! The house shattered into a million pieces. Just like you see in the movies. It was the shit.

As it turned out Pretty Boy and his woman weren't even home. They'd escaped downtown to some cheap motel. After that day I never saw Pretty Boy again.

Now, the girl down in Highland Park, who I had told not to say anything and who's life I had saved, went and told the police on Jackie. So the police came down to the hood and scooped up Jackie who stayed on Tuxedo.

Man what some people will do under pressure. The police scared Jackie so bad that she told on everybody. She gave her brother's name; Leroy, my name and Parhoo's name. So, after that, I went to Highland Park to stay with Portia. I figured they wouldn't look for me there, 'cause I stayed in Detroit and I felt like they wouldn't figure I would go to Highland Park where the crime had taken place and I was right. It wasn't long though, before the police picked up Parhoo and then Leroy.

While I was hidin' out in Highland Park, I hooked up with these guys named Burgundy Bow and Dent. I'd met Dent through Block. Block had did a bit from an armed robbery we did in 1972. It was me, Block and D.J. And as usual, Sid The Kid was the driver. What had happened was that we went and stuck-up an after-hours house and took some jewelry and money. The way Block got caught was he was upstairs stashin'. In other words he gave me a t.v., some jewelry and told me to go downstairs and while I was down there he was stashin' shit with the intent of keepin' it for himself. So by him stayin' up there so long he ended up gettin' busted. What happened was we'd cut the music off and the people downstairs heard what was goin' on and called the police.

As soon as I'd put the stuff in the car with the Kid,

the police shot around the corner. The next thang I knew, me and the Kid were pullin' off and Black Joe, who'd set the robbery up, was still down the block watchin' from a real safe distance, 'cause from the distance he was from, there was no way he was gone get caught. So that's how Block ended up in prison and meetin' Dent, who was from the Jeffrey projects.

Dent had already been in the joint for some years when Block got there and by Block's father havin' money Block ended up gettin' out on an appeals bond, and as it turned out they both ended up gettin' out at about the same time.

Being that I was still on the run for murder, I stopped slangin' altogether because that would have caused me to have to be stationary. So instead, I started doin' stick-up's. I stuck-up from June 1973 to the late part of 1974. Robbin' banks became my new hustle. It was me, Burgundy Bow, my man Raymond (Baby Ray) People's brother Nate the Great-both of whom are dead now, and Dent.

Nate the Great had a lot of motherfuckin' heart. There was nothin' he wouldn't do when it came to commitin' crimes.

In terms of the robberies, me and Nate would go into the bank with the note, hand it to the ever so nervous teller, get the money and run out. Simple as that. We never robbed the whole bank, just the tellers.

One day, right around this same period of time we all rode down to the Fox Theater to watch the movie

Willie Dynamite. That's when the Fox use to show movies all the time. Block had a 1973 Mark IV. Gold, sharp as hell. By this time I was usin' fake I.D. 'cause like I said I was still on the run for murder. The name I was using was Alonso Fergurson.

So, after we got down to the Fox, I saw this guy I know name Skip outta' Highland Park. Skip was Faye's brother, one of Portia's friends. Altogether there was Skip, Darcell, and Vera. So we all spoke and then sat down to watch the movie.

The next thang you know these guys name Bay Bay and Papa' Dupree out of the Brewster Projects was fightin' with some people and tearin' shit up. Come to think of it that's one of the reason's it ain't no movie theater's in downtown Detroit 'cause everybody used to use 'em as boxin' rings.

I didn't know Papa Dupree at the time but I would later meet him and we would become the best of friends.

After we left the Fox, everybody jumped into their cars and headed north on Woodward.

Fat Skip, Darcell, and Vera was in one car, and me and Block was in another car. All a sudden, me and Fat Skip, not thinkin' that the police were still lookin' for me just started racin'. We raced down Woodward and we weren't stoppin' for nothin'. We had to be going about eighty to ninety miles per hour . The regular speed limit is like 35mph.

The next thang I knew all you could see were flashin' blue and red lights behind us. But we still wasn't pullin' over, 'cause I knew if I did I was busted. So I drove faster.

We raced for about three more miles before the police were able to stop us. What they did was at Woodward and Clairmount, right there by Northern High School, they set up a police barricade that was unlike any I'd ever seen. I mean they had that shit set up like Fort Knox or something. It musta' been about twenty cop cars out there. All with their lights flashin'. So with no where else to go, we pulled over and off to jail I went. They took me and Skip to jail, because we were the drivers and let everybody else go.

When we got to jail we gave 'em our licenses and they ran a fingerprint check on each of us. Throughout the months prior to this day I had been tryna' mess up my fingerprints, so if I ever got pulled over they wouldn't know it was me. And I was also usin' the fake I.D. I got from Dent so I felt like I was goin' home shortly so I wasn't worried about nothin'. I called Portia, who was nine months pregnant with our son Mo Mo, and told her that I would be home shortly and to have dinner ready when I got there. This was January 17, 1974.

About four hours later, they called Skip and told him he could go. Then they called, "Alonso Fergurson", I jumped up smilin', then they said "A.K.A. Butch Jones." Man my heart just dropped. I couldn't see nothin' but bars in my future. I was fucked up. The next thang I knew, the Highland Park Police was there to pick me up and ten days later I was being arraigned for murder.

When we got to court, Linda testified that I shot the guy and that my partner Leroy stabbed him. She also testified that we raped her. But that was a lie. She only said that because the boy who had gotten killed sister thought she had somethin' to do with it and had threatened to kill her. They also told her if she didn't go to court and testify that they would kill her.

Now, they had all four of us in custody. Parhoo and Jackie were taken to court first. They were taken to court around February or March of '74.

Now get this. Parhoo who didn't do nothin' but go with us to the place, was convicted of second degree murder and got life in prison.

Jackie took a plea and she got ten to fifteen for manslaughter.

Leroy, who actually killed the guy, took a plea and got three to fifteen.

My future didn't look to bright for me at this point.

While I was locked up my brother got killed in the process of a stick-up. And because I had spent my money as fast as I was makin' it, my mother got me an attorney named Sheldon Helpburn from the proceeds of my brother's life insurance policy. Ironically, on the same day that my brother was killed, my son Mo Mo was born. The date was January 31, 1974. My mother said, "The Lord took one and brought another into the world." That's how we always looked at it. So when my son was born, I gave him *his* middle name. Anyway, I got this excellent attorney, named Sheldon Helpburn and that's the only reason I didn't get life.

When Sheldon Helpburn came down to the jail he wrote on a piece of paper 'win' and circled it. He then said, "That's the only thing I'm interested in, is winning."

He asked was I prepared to sit in jail while he fought the case.

I said, "I'll sit down here two or three years. I just don't wanna' get life like my codefendant Parhoo did."

So, he said, "Alright."

I ended up stayin' in the County Jail from January 17, 1974 'til March 22, 1975. That's when I got sentenced. I took a manslaughter plea and got seven and a half to fifteen.

Two days after my sentencin', I was bein' quarantined in Jackson prison.

The guys had been preparin' me for my stay in Jackson, but you can never get prepared for Jackson. At night they make all these crazy noises. Any kinda' animal noise you can think of they make in Jackson. You see, you ain't suppose ta' talk, so when the lights go out everybody start makin' all kinds of bird and cat noises, and start barkin' like dogs, anythang ta' aggravate the guards.

Anyway, I stayed in quarantine for twenty-one days and then they sent me to a place called the Hill. The Hill was the Ionia, Michigan reformatory. It was a real rough place for guys who were teenagers.

Now, mind you, I had never been locked up before except for my time in the County Jail. So there was a lot I had to learn about being locked up.

While I was in the County Jail, I ended up meetin' a lot of people and one of them turned out to be Papa Dupree; the one I told you about back at the Fox. Anyway, to make a long story short, I got into a fight back at the County 'cause this guy called himself takin' my donuts after I had slept in one mornin'. See I was taught that the only thing that should be taken was medicine. But since homeboy didn't believe in that philosophy I had to beat him upside his mothafuckin' head.

Anyway, Papa Dupree liked my style and we became friends. So when we were both shipped to the hill together, that was cool. Ain't nothin' like bein' in prison and knowin' you got at least one real friend in there with you.

Like me, Papa Dupree had also received fifteen years for manslaughter. It was for the death of this guy named Hairman. Papa didn't kill 'em, but him and a friend of mine named X was with the guy who did, so both of 'em got time outta' it.

A few years passed and before I knew it, it was 1975. Cool and the Gang had just came out with the record 'Summer Madness' and me, Ben Kencade, Papa Dupree, and a whole bunch of other guys were all out in the yard. We had told a bunch of guys that when they called 'lockup' not to go in, 'cause we were gonna' protest for all the bullshit the prison system was takin'us through. So, when it came time for the yard to go in everybody should just hold their ground.

When the whistles blew, everybody started lookin' at one another like fuck the authorities. Then after a few minutes everybody got real serious and somebody shouted, "Hey, let's go over to H block." They had an H block and a J block. The H block was on the first floor where they kept all the prisoners in temporary custody. (The snitches and the sissies.) So, we went over to H block and took it over. They fucked all the sissies, stabbed a coupla' white boy snitches, and busted all their stuff up. Then we sat there stuff on fire.

When the institution saw what was goin' on ,they brought the riot squad in to tear-gas us. They didn't want to come in shootin' 'cause they didn't want anybody in protective custody to get killed.

While all of this was goin' on the inmates had this sissy named China Doll, who had this real big butt, down there tearin' that ass up. To them that ass was like a ripe juicy pussy. Those guys lost their minds.

Everybody was in line waitin' a turn at that ass. I'm tellin' you, it don't pay ta' be no faggot in the joint. Or weak minded for that matter 'cause they get it too.

Na' just for the record, I didn't have nothin' ta' do wit' no butt fuckin' an' shit, 'cause faggots ain't never been my thang, you know. So let the whole world know, I like real pussy too much.

We ended up runnin' outta' H block and goin' to J block.

After we finished in H Block, we ran over to J

Block. That's where all the guys from the west side of Detroit bunked.

When we got over to J block, we tried to barricade the doors so the guards couldn't get in. So, they started shootin' tear-gas through the windows. They tear-gassed the whole J block and couldn't nobody breathe or see. Then this guy just hollered, "Put your head in the toilet and flush it. Wet your towels and put it over your eyes, so the tear gas won't mess your eyes up." All a sudden all these toilets immediately started flushin'.

We took over for about two hours. Then it took 'em about four to six more hours to get the institution right again and during this process about five more sissies got ganged raped and stabbed. But it was nothin' like what happened to China Doll. About fifteen people in a row fucked China Doll. When he got to protective custody he had to get I don't know how many stitches to sew his ass up. In all, about two hundred people participated in the riot.

From that day on, they started lettin' the guys come out more, use the phones, have more property, and have more products to choose from in the stores. Technically, we wanted more black products. That riot in 1975 in Ionia, Michigan changed the whole State prison system.

All while we was up in Ionia, I met a lot of good guys. Hard tough, guys that would kill you at the drop of a hat or a blink of an eye. These guys became my friends. You know, even though I had no problems with being locked up 'cause like I said I was a real one and didn't mind doin' my time if I'd done the crime, but the one thing I would always think about, was why in the fuck did I have to go over to Highland Park in the first place. I could have just given Parhoo the gun and let him take care of his business. Instead a person ended up dead, people ended up gettin' long prison terms, and quite frankly, that's one time I could have avoided going to prison.

Chapter 3

Y.B.I.

When I came home in 1978 I was ready, 'cause in spite of everything, all I could think about while I was up the way was gettin' money. I had no choice but to think about gettin' money. I knew the dope game better than anybody else my age. That's what I knew, so that's what I was going back to. So anyway when they opened up those prison gates on February 11, 1978 and Portia and Nate the Great picked me up, I was ready to take it to the limit.

As soon as we got to Martindale we cruised down the street to let everybody know. "He's baaa'ack!" Then I hooked up with my man Block and all my homies. The one thing that had tripped me out was how big everybody had gotten. Now compared to the way I was before I went to jail I had gotten big, but compared to most of them, I was small, but I was in shape. I weighed about 180 pounds solid, due to my cross trainin' regime of runnin' and liftin' weights while in the joint.

After a few days I settled into the swing of things, got me a haircut and began my mission to become what was to become the biggest money makin' enterprise by any Black man on any street in America.

How it started was about a month after I got home, I went down to Cousins Shoe Store and while I was down there I ran into this guy named Milwaukee Jack. I had known him from my days of hangin' at the Chess and Cue. I told him I'd takin' a rap and we talked a little about life and then exchanged numbers. He would later become a springboard to where I was destined to go.

In the meantime, me, Block and Baby Ray was watchin' heroin sell like wild flower all around us. Compared to how it was before I went to the joint, a lot more people was sellin' raw, so I knew we had to take it to the next level. So, I told my boys that we were gonna' go on our street, which was Monterey and set up shop. I had never really had a big package of heroin before. The most I ever had on me at once was an ounce, which consisted of twenty-eight grams.

When I was ready, I called Milwaukee Jack and he put me down like four flat tires. He came through and gave me four ounces of some strong heroin. We got it tested and it was takin' about a ten. When I speak of a ten that means that I can take one quarter of raw and put ten quarters of cut on it. For every seven grams I could put seventy grams on it.

So in 1978 we started sellin' mixtures. The mixtures consisted of quinine, dormus, and lactose. To make the heroin stronger we stopped usin' lactose and used straight quinine and dormus. Now again, just for the record. These was hard-core dope fiends that was shootin' this shit up and they didn't give a fuck. It wasn't no kids or nothin' like that, nor did little kids sell our shit for us. All of that shit about lil' eight and nine year old kids sellin' for us was nothin' but a myth.

Man you had to see the way them people was respondin' to that raw. For example, before we moved our hustle to other neighborhoods, the Dexter bus would stop right at the corner of Dexter and Monterey and about fifty people would get off the bus. All lookin' for heroin.

Also it use to be so tight for the police that they even use to ride the buses and jump off in order to try ta' raid us. At the time what they were doing was known as a blitz. But after the first time of them doing that shit, we was ready for them and we started puttin' our lookouts on the buses right along with everybody else.

After awhile, I decided that the shit was sellin' so good that it was time to take the blow which we were stampin' Y.B.I. and introduce it to the downtown area. Wasn't no need in all those people from downtown catchin' the buses to us. It wasn't nothin' for us to take it to them.

Exclusive in Detroit: Kid dealers

By Lowell Cauffiel
News Staff Writer

Detroit is the only major U.S. city where upper-level heroin operators use regiments of juveniles to peddle drugs on the street.

Though New York, Los Angeles, Chicago, Cleveland and Washington have similar conditions which could sprout such organized networks, Detroit has a unique problem with teen heroin-peddling organizations like Young Boys Inc.

"There's the occasional youth used for transport of drugs but we haven't seen anything like what you have in Detroit," said Insp. Dennis Ryan, head of the police narcotics unit in New York.

"But I'm sure it's not far off for us. Word tends to spread quickly in this business."

Added Martin McDonough, a detective in Cleveland's narcotics unit: "That could be a real problem here with juveniles. Conditions certainly are right. McDonald's advertised for a couple of jobs here and 600 kids

Continued on Page 6A

Basically, at this time the Y.B.I. consisted of a lot of guys from the tenth precinct area. Which was our neighborhood. There were numerous guys who were a part of the organization, so there is no way that I can mention them all. So, what I will do is mention those that I can remember as being there from day one and who became many of the lieutenants.

The crew included Mickey, Baby Ray, W.W., Butch, Rod, Butchie, Andre, Frankenstein, Jerry Berry, Paul Bunion, Gene Hackman, Tyrone, Chuck, Fat Steve and his brother Brat, Mark Webb, Mark Jones, Sand Man, Kirk McGurk, Quick Kirk, Richie Rich, Dead Eye, Sid the Kid, Danny Boy, Rerun, Tyson, Slim, Fat Herbie, Minute Man, Farod, 50, Little Crusher, Big Crusher out the projects, Crooked Mouth Mike, Dick Tracey, Little Teddy, Arty Art, Arty Art's brother Blair, Rickey Peoples and Billy Peoples who were no relation, and Buster. All of these guys were the heart of the Young Boys. Not to mention Stony Rony and Dart Bart. These guys was the foundation of Young Boys Incorporated. We was the ones who went all over the city and held it down. The fifty of us could go anywhere in the city, bust a spot open, and hold it down without any problems.

If we had a problem, we had a group that consisted of the wreckin' crew. I was elected to be in charge of the wreckin' crew. Basically, it was me, Butchie, Terrible, Moe Heart, Dead Eye, Quick Kirk, and Richie Rich. There wasn't a problem too big or too small.

April 11, 1982 •

Only in Detroit: Kids deal

Continued from Page 1A

showed up."

NEW YORK's organized crime unit contacted the federal Drug Enforcement Administration office in Detroit early last week to learn more about the problem.

Narcotics detectives agree that certain conditions have encouraged the rise of operations such as Young Boys Inc. They include:

- High unemployment among inner-city youths, which boosts the money incentive for joining a drug-dealing network.
- A juvenile justice system that fails to punish or rehabilitate young dealers, thereby assuring that the young offender will be back on the streets shortly after he's caught.
- A steady supply of heroin into the city, financed by kingpins who use juveniles to peddle heroin to addicts

As in Detroit, law enforcement officials in other cities say their juvenile justice system appears inadequate to cope with today's juvenile criminals.

"Our juveniles are being protected here by juvenile laws that are very much antiquated," said Chicago Police Cmdr. Leroy Martin, chief of the city's narcotics unit.

"They were not written for the youth of the 1980s. We're trying to deal with juveniles that are committing adult crimes."

MARTIN SAID that Chicago is beginning to see gangs like the Latin Counts and the Black Gangster Disciples selling heroin and oth. r drugs. But they operate out of schoolyards, selling drugs to other youths, not adults.

What's more, until two years ago, Martin said, these gangs were strictly in the "shakedown business"; collecting money on bad debts for drug dealers and loan sharks.

"Their dealing operations might have caught on from Detroit because it just started recently and there is some communication between the two cities," Martin said. "It's been proven in Detroit to be a very effective way of dealing drugs and minimizing arrest."

While Young Boys Inc. has operated in Detroit since early 1978, the group received widespread attention after a teen believed to be connected to Young Boys was charged last month in the fatal shooting of a Detroit police officer and the wounding of his partner.

SUBSEQUENT stories about Young Boys have created some confusion and myths about its origins and size, police say.

Even undercover narcotics officers admit that much of their intelligence on the group is "speculation."

One police theory is that the organization was able to take hold after a crackdown on several long-time heroin czars, including Frank Lee Usher, who is now serving a life sentence for the triple beheading of three people in a drug dispute.

But that theory also is disputed. Narcotics officers admit privately that there are so many top-level operators in the business that they don't know the extent of Detroit's heroin network.

"I think we just see the tip of the iceberg," said one.

While Young Boys Inc. apparently started in 1978 in the west side's 10th (Livernois) Precinct, there are many separate organizations with similar methods of operation.

ONE LONG-TIME 10th Precinct youth officer said juveniles have told him that there now are three separate organizations in that precinct alone.

"Everybody caught on the street is being called YBI," said Insp. Raymond Murray, Detroit police narcotics chief. "Well, that's a lot of bull. We do not have just one organization handling all the drug dealing in this city."

The original YBI organization has made an aggressive effort to expand beyond the 10th precinct to at least 15 other locations around the city and neighboring Highland Park, police say.

IN 1978, FOR instance, a group of YBI dealers tried to take over drug operations in the John R. and Erskine area — a location with a 20-year history for drug sales.

The teens were run out by long-time dealers there, Murray said. But they returned the next day with other youths armed with baseball bats and beat up their competitors, thus enabling them to take over traffic in the nearby Brewster housing project, Murray said.

The organization recently set up operations in the Jeffries project. Narcotics police say projects are ideal trafficking locations because the young sellers can have lookouts in high-rise buildings and escape quickly into the buildings during an arrest attempt.

But Young Boys Inc., or organizations like it, do not have a monopoly on drug trafficking in the city, police say.

INSTEAD, THEY appear to be a new twist on the more traditional ways of marketing heroin, such as the dope house or "shooting gallery" where addicts visit a house and inject the drug on the spot.

"The police department alone is not going solve the heroin problem," said Murray. "I'm not so sure the criminal justice system alone can solve the problem. Drug addiction is a social problem as much as anything."

The heroin dealing by teens — most of whom use their profits for material goods rather than drugs — falls into the same category.

Said one Third Precinct youth division officer who has dealt with dozens of the young pushers: "You know I'm really not so sure that if I lived in one of those rat traps in the projects, had no job had a mother on welfare and saw all the materialism that this country glorifies that I wouldn't be out there dealing myself."

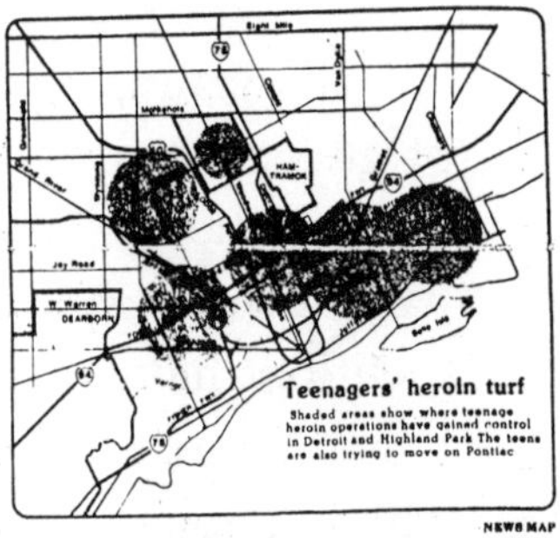

Teenagers' heroin turf

Shaded areas show where teenage heroin operations have gained control in Detroit and Highland Park The teens are also trying to move on Pontiac

NEWS MAP

war, humor

What made us so strong was that we were all dedicated to puttin' down the mixtures at that particular time. No matter what, we put it down from sun up to sun down, and the police couldn't do nothin' about it.

They had this one police officer named Gerald Benacki who worked central narcotics and he along with three other officers; Popeye, Whicker and Rocky Mountain Red (McNamara) were determined to break the Young Boys. They put their total life into it. They knew every young boy and everything. But it would be years before they would even make a dent on what we were doing.

Just in that short period of time after I came home, sales skyrocketed 100%. We controlled eighty to ninety percent of the heroin bein' sold in Detroit. Other crews, like Pony Down tried to compete, but for the most part, there was simply no competition. None.

The Young Boys started doin' ten thousand a day, then twenty thousand and before you knew it, by 1981 fifty thousand a day.

We had gotten so big that a few of us leaders kinda split into different groups. Baby Ray had a crew, W.W. had a crew and I had a crew.

I took all the hard-core people with me. It was like I had a baseball team and I had all the hitters on my team.

Baby Ray and W.W. had all the catchers on their team. What ended up happenin' was that even though I didn't start the organization all by myself, I did eventually end up taken over the entire operation. If it were to go to the next level, somebody had to do it, so why not me.

By this time, central narcotics was having meetings downtown everyday. Their slogan became "Let's get Butch Jones. Let's get Butch Jones." Everyday they were raidin' and tryna' bust my crew. But they wasn't really gettin' nothin'.

Also about this time in 1981, my friend Fat George introduced me to a fine lady named Betty. At this particular time Betty was goin' with this guy called Pimpin' D. And together they sold drugs.

Pimpin' D. and Betty made a lot of money together, but the problem was, everytime they would make it, D. would smoke it up. This was about the time crack came out. Anyway they had this nice ass crib over on Archdale so they was hangin' a little, but like I said he was mostly fuckin' up the money.

Betty forever bein' on top of her game, saw that I had my shit on strong so she came to me with a proposition: Give her a hundred thousand dollars and she'll cop me some of the strongest stuff I ever seen. Mind you, I didn't really know her, but I'm a businessman, ya' know. And plus a hundred thousand dollars which is what she asked for was the equivalent to me of what fifty dollars is to most of you, cause like I said, the organization was doing about fifty thousand a day at this time so a hundred thousand wasn't know real big deal to me.

So I gave her the money and she made it happen. She went to New York to see the people she knew and the next thang I knew, I was sellin' the strongest heroin ever brought in to Detroit, period.

After D. got wind of what Betty had did for me, he got mad. He went and took all of Betty's furniture out of her house, all the silverware, and even the knick-knacks off the wall.

When I got to Betty's house and saw her and the kids were sleepin' on the floor I really got mad because I knew he'd done it on the strength of his dislike for me.

It was at that point that I tracked down D and said, "Nigga you know how the game goes, yo' hoe chose me, what's up?"He told me he wasn't honorin' the game and he didn't respect that shit and we could go to war.

So I said, "Okay nigga, it's on. If you want war then you got it."

I waited until Halloween rolled around and I said to myself, okay, now it's time to get him.

I dressed up like Darth Vador and went over to D.'s house, 'cause I felt like it was time for me to holler at the punk, you know since that's the way he wanted it. But when I got to his house the nigga wasn't there.

So, me and my woman Betty went on ahead to a Halloween party and hometeam got to live another day.

It's kinda crazy how me and Betty just hooked up like that 'cause after all I still had a wife. But you know, I was out there and I wasn't thinkin' like that. I figured I was a king and a king could have as many wives as he wanted. It was no real disrespect to my wife 'cause that's just the life I was livin' at the time. I felt at the time that I was still treatin' my wife real good, I was taken care of my kids and my wife was my right hand man. But Betty was my left. The only thing I regret is I should have just stayed true blue to just my wife, but like I said that was a different time and a different me. A hundred thousand dollars a day will make you think like you control the world. I only wish just a fraction of you could experience what it's like then you'd understand what I mean.

When D. found out that the Young Boys was lookin' for him, he flipped totally out. He went an' turned straight dope fiend. Word got back to me that he was hidin' out somewhere in some apartment with a bunch of other dope fiends smokin' dope an' shit, so I said fuck it, I ain't got time to be chasin' no dope fiends, so I just put him on the back burner and went on with my life. With Betty.

Now that me and Betty was going together, my business went from fifty thousand a day to one hundred thousand a day. I had a money-counter over on Archdale and unless I'd counted one hundred thousand a day I wasn't interested in shutin' down.

Everyday me, Betty and Baby Ray's younger brother Timmie Peoples would start counting the money. As soon as we'd get to one hundred thousand that's when we'd shut down. I would put word out that it was time to shut down and everybody would come to the house and have big fun, 'cause like I said, we was one big cold hearted family, the fifty of us.

By the early part of 1982 that's when the police really started tryna' bring us down. I mean they were not holdin' back any punches. I remember it clear because it hadn't been long since Milwaukee had introduced me to Sylvester (Seals) Murray. Or S Man which we called him.

S Man was introduced to me as the guy who could keep me supplied, 'cause, at this time, I was sellin' heroin at an all time high. We had blows called C.B.S., Hoochie Con, and Murder One. These were some of the names under which we used to get money.

Now that I'd met up with S Man that was just another avenue by which I could get kilos and that was just what I needed. It was nearly impossible to make millions without being able to get my hands on as many kilos as I could get.

He began supplyin' me one or two kilos at a time, but just that quick we'd even outgrown what he was capable of supplyin'. So lucky for me, I had not burned any bridges and still had Betty goin' to New York and Milwaukee Jack goin' to Chicago, California and any other place he could to keep me supplied.

The organization was stronger than ever. We didn't take no shit off nobody. Anybody who got in our way ended up in the dirt. It wasn't no ifs, ands, or buts about it. No shakin' and fakin'. We took care of our business.

It got so bad that Central narcotics was runnin' so much overtime on tryna' stop us, that eventually they had to give up and lay off many of their officers.

They ended up applyin' for a federal grant from the United States government in order to combat us.

At this particular time, Ronald and Nancy Reagan was in the White House. Nancy Reagan, who'd come up with the campaign slogan, "Just Say No To Drugs," came to Detroit to visit and by the time she left, Young Boy's Inc., was her number one target. She'd gotten information that we were sellin' drugs to children, which was a lie, but that's all she needed to hear.

After she got back to Washington, in no time at all, a task force was sent back to Detroit to hunt us down and break up Young Boys Incorporated.

Word quickly spread that me and S Man was their number one target and they would not stop until Young Boy's Inc. was finished.

But my attitude was, What the fuck was the federal government tryna' arrest me for. I hadn't broken not one federal law. All I was doin' was sellin' ten dollar packs. I hadn't gone outta' town and bought no drugs. I hadn't crossed no State lines. I hadn't discussed drug transactions on the phone. I hadn't done none of the things that would consist of commitin' a federal crime, but yet I was under federal investigation.

You see, the government does shit like that. They think they can do whatever they want because they're the government. They've been doin' shit like that ever since slavery. They just pop up with shit. Here I was, merely committin' State crimes, and they were just gone

Detroit vital to Reagan's war on crime

WASHINGTON — President Reagan announced an assault on organized crime and drug trafficking, naming Detroit as the site of one of 12 new regional anti crime task forces.

The centerpiece of the administration's plan, which was announced yesterday, is the shifting of about 1,000 experienced federal agents and prosecutors to Detroit and 11 other major cities. The program will cost between $160 million and $200 million a year.

Calling organized crime the "dark, evil enemy within," the president said the administration will do "what is necessary to end the drug menace and cripple

Continued on Page 9A

Detroit named in crime war

Continued from Page 1A

organized crime."

"As all of you know," the president said in a speech at the Justice Department, "crime today is an American epidemic. It takes the lives of over 20,000 Americans a year, it touches nearly a third of American homes and results in about $8.8 billion a year in financial losses."

MR. REAGAN SAID organized crime reaches into every part of society, including law enforcement and public office. "The American people want the mob and its associates brought to justice and its power broken," he declared.

He called the new program "a major initiative that I believe can mark a turning point in the battle against crime."

Under the plan, sophisticated equipment and technology will be supplied to the task forces and 11 prisons would be expanded to hold 1,260 additional inmates, the White House said.

The president created a Cabinet-level commission to coordinate federal efforts and keep the president informed of problems.

The program also calls for establishing a national center to train local law enforcement agents to combat such relatively new organized crime ventures as arson, bombing, bribery, computer theft, contract fraud and bid-rigging, as well as drug smuggling.

NEW AGENTS would be hired to replace those transferred to the task forces.

The new teams will be in addition to the

force a federal crime on me. Either we have laws or we don't. What I was doing was commitin' State crimes but in fact what the government was actually sayin' was; you're too big for the State so we're gonna' have to take over from here. Law or no law. We'll make up one as we go along.

Anyway, by this time I had come out with a blow called Check Mate. I called it check mate in honor of my love for the game of chess and the significance of the term "Check mate" which means "The winner". And as far as I was concerned, that's what I had done. Won!

I bought so many luxury items during this time that it was crazy. Imagine, well I'm sure you can. A hundred thousand a day. One of the items I bought which I got the most pride out of was a gray Vette, I called it the Gray Ghost. Man it was cold. A chromed up, '82 cross fire. I was so happy about the car that I decided to join the Vette club, but can you believe they wouldn't let me in. Talkin' 'bout they don't know me. I guess you had to be some uppity mothafucka or somethin', I don't know, but I simply said fuck it, I ain't kissin' nobody's ass.

So I made my own Vette club, you know. I went out and made a deal with Jim Shay over at Executive Motors on Van Dyke to buy one new Vette everyday for twenty thousand dollars flat. I didn't have no credit, so everythang I bought, I bought straight out with flat out cash. Money, taxes and all.

The first day I went over there I bought a blue, black, and brown Vette from him. Then I bought another four from S Man who also had his own dealership. After I got my whole crew all hooked up I then went out and bought me a Benz, a Jag and a Porche. I gave the Porche to my wife for her birthday.

After I got a lil' tired of those cars, S Man referred me over to Don Massey's Cadillac. While there I talked to Bob Dotley and he showed me this stainless steel car whose doors opened up like wings called the De'Lorian. Now that car was the shit. Detroit Piston Isiah Thomas was the first one to have one in the State of Michigan and I was intent on not being too far behind.

So I test drove it and after I got back I asked the guy, "If I buy it can I get it today?" And he said yeah. So I asked him how much it cost and he told me twenty-five thousand, so without hesitation I went out to the car and bam! retrieved the twenty-five thousand and gave it to him. He then asked whose name I wanted the car in and I told him Nelson's Flower shop, 'cause I had gone into business with my auntie Ms. Nelson. So, I purchased the car as an agent of the flower shop.

Basically, I did it to boost the business of the flowershop. And it worked. People used to marvel at that car because at the time it was like a futuristic type car so everybody use to really stare at it and end up going in the shop and buying something.

Man, when I first got into the car after I bought it I was foolin' like a mothafucka. I had the doors spread wide open and the music blastin' as loud as it could go and all of a sudden I look up and who do I see–the police.

Teenage High Rollers On Detroit Drug Scene

Detroit

A 15-year-old boy recently walked into a suburban Mercedes-Benz showroom, pointed to a black 500 SEL and announced, "I'll take it." He paid with $62,000 cash from a brown paper bag.

In the Jeffries Housing Project on the east side, teenagers are driving new Corvettes, Christmas bonuses for jobs well done.

According to federal and local authorities, these youths are

A police officer said one leader of the operation 'gave out 16 Corvettes for all the kids to ride around in'

"runners" for narcotics rings that supply the city's estimated 50,000 addicts.

Robert De Fauw, head of the local office of the federal Drug Enforcement Administration, said, "We have a unique phenomenon in Detroit in that groups of children as young as 12 years old are being recruited to work in drug rings where they can make as much as $2000 to $5000 a week."

David Hoover, speaking for the agency in Washington, agreed. "Nowhere else in the country have we found so many juveniles involved in such highly structured heroin gangs," he said.

James Tishuck, a Detroit narcotics officer, said: "Despite all we do, it's going to be impossible to stop gangs from recruiting these kids. It is a matter of economics.

"You're 12 years old, living in a Detroit housing project, your parents are out of work, and some guy in a fancy car comes by and tells you he can help you make $300 a day. You're going to listen."

However, local law-enforcement agencies have taken these actions against heroin-trafficking rings that employ children and teenagers on the streets:

■ A special force of local narcotics officers and federal drug enforcement agents has been formed to concentrate on heroin rings. It is financed by the Justice Department to buy drugs, reward informers and pay Detroit officers' overtime.

■ A two-year investigation of Young Boys Inc., a group that police say employed 300 young people to sell $350,000 worth of heroin a week, has resulted in 32 convictions and the confiscation of $1.5 million in cash, found in garbage bags.

■ Investigations of Pony Down and Adidas, two heroin rings that employ many of the youths who were in Young Boys Inc., are under way.

According to federal affidavits, recruiting the young for drug trafficking was the idea of 28-year-old Milton David Jones. The papers show that Jones left prison in the winter of 1980, after serving a manslaughter sentence for a killing when he was 17, and began assembling groups of young boys from the Montrey-Dexter neighborhood.

Assistant U.S. Attorney Robert Morgan said Jones would "stand before these kids in a playground and preach to them that he would get them high on money, jewelry and clothes if they worked for him. He promised to make them millionaires."

Last May, when Jones was sentenced to 12 years in jail for tax offenses and engaging in a continual criminal enterprise, he had 300 youths selling $50,000 worth of heroin a day, prosecutors said.

The hierarchical, almost corporate structure of Young Boys Inc. was said to have been devised by Jones and 30-year-old Sylvester Murray, identified by police as the ring's chief supplier of drugs. Both the Pony Down and Adidas gangs, which took their names from the athletic shoes their members wore, used Young Boys Inc. as a model for their organizations.

As outlined by police and by Wayne County prosecutors, Young Boys Inc. operated this way:

The leaders of the gang would take raw heroin to a "hookup" house where a half-dozen people would, like an assembly line, mix the heroin with sugar and quinine.

The mix would be spooned into coin envelopes that would be stamped "Murder One" or "Rolls-Royce," the street drugs' brand names. Ten of these envelopes would be grouped in a "bundle." Early in the morning, the "bundles" would be taken by the youths to where the drugs would be sold.

Each such location, usually a street corner or a public housing project, was supervised by a "top dog" who would distribute the envelopes to runners, the lowest and usually the youngest participants.

The runners would sell an envelope to an addict for $13. From this, the organization would receive $10; the runner would get the other $3 as his fee, or "tops."

"If a kid wanted to hustle," said Tishuck, "his 'tops' could come to $300 or $400 a day. That's why, when we found an 11-year-old carrying two grand in his pocket, we weren't surprised."

According to prosecutors' papers and wiretaps, Sunday was generally payday. All would gather in a downtown warehouse and be paid salaries according to their positions, in addition to their "tops." Bonuses were frequent.

"They would take these kids on trips to Las Vegas and show them things they had only just dreamed of," De Fauw said.

New York Times

After I pulled over they walked slowly up to the car like I was Bat Man or somethin'. "Damn Butch," one of the officers said, "What kinda car you got now?" My reply was, "Look, why don't ya'll gone and take it around the block?" And they said, "They didn't want the feds to see them ridin' around in my car." But if not for that, they woulda' done it.

See in the 10th precinct all the police officers knew who I was. I had superstar status. I didn't have no problems with the blue an' whites over there.

The De'Lorian was a nice car in concept but overall it turned out to be a lemon. The car use to cut off on me all the time and so I gave it to my wife thinkin' some how she would have better luck with it, but after it cut off on her on the freeway she didn't want any parts of it either, so I ended up tradin' it in for another Vette.

Chapter 4

Making Money

By the summer of 1982 it was time for the real Vette club to go into action. Our first trip was planned for the Cedar Point amusement park located in Sandusky, Ohio. It was planned that everybody would meet up on Louise and 12th in Highland Park and that we would wear our colors. Red and White. Red for the blood and white for China white, which we were sellin'. By this time, I had purchased about nineteen or twenty Vettes. The caravan was so awesome that the press wrote about it.

Altogether, including some of our other cars there were roughly eighty cars headed down the freeway.

Before we went to Cedar Point, we all went out to Footlocker. We was about forty deep. On that day alone

I went out and spent about twelve thousand dollars in one whop. Then the next day I went back and spent another nine thousand. It wasn't nothin' to go to the mall and get whatever we wanted.

I know some of you probably thinkin', "What about the dope houses? Who was holdin' down the fort?" Well we took care of that. While we were gone we had other guys holdin' down the fort for us. No matter where we went, we always had somebody holdin' down the spots, ya' know.

Anyway when we got to the freeway we was holdin' the west side down baby! Man, we was flyin' down the freeway with those flat-top John Dillinger hats on like we owned the mothafucka, just talkin' on our cellular phones just foolin'. Man we took over the freeway that day. And check, the police wasn't nowhere to be found and if they was, they must've got specific orders not to mess with the Y.B.I. At least that's the way we felt about.

We were so disciplined in everythang we did. We was organized. A bunch of professional slangers and hitters is what it boiled down to. The government was gettin' more and more pissed off by the day.

One day they ran up in S Man's apartment, down in the Jeffersonian and took eight hundred and fifty thousand dollars from him and this guy name Darryl.

S Man told me they actually took nine hundred grand but you know how that is. After a raid its always some discrepancy about what the amount really is. Some of the money was always comin' up missin'. Anyway S

Jeffersonian raid nets drug supplier suspect

By Jim Tittsworth
News Staff Writer

A suspected major supplier of Detroit heroin trafficking operations — including Young Boys Inc. — was arrested last night at his apartment in the luxury Jeffersonian Apartments on Detroit's near east side.

Detroit police and federal drug enforcement agents seized about three pounds of suspected heroin and $820,000 in cash from two apartments in the 8 p.m. raid, said Robert DeFauw, head of the DEA in Detroit.

"This was definitely a major supplier of heroin in this area and it is going to hurt several inner-city drug operations. It will have a tremendous impact on Young Boys Inc. and others," DeFauw said.

Armed with federal search warrants, federal agents and Detroit narcotics officers raided two apartments in the Jeffersonian, one of the 24th floor and the other on the 27th floor.

The man arrested rented the apartment on the 27th floor, DeFauw said. A Smith & Wesson 9mm semi-automatic pistol also was found inside the apartment, said DeFauw.

Police officials said the arrest and seizure is part of an eight-month investigation by Detroit police and the DEA.

More arrests are expected from the investigation, officers said.

Man told me it was his connects money, so that was one day that the feds did make a decent sting, cause right after that, S Man began complainin' about money.

Right about this time I'd bought a house in Oak Park. The house had a swimming pool in the backyard and I had a big balloon installed around it which allowed me to swim anytime of the year. What the balloon did was' keep the pool at eighty to ninety degrees year round. So when my friends came to my house they could go swimmin', even in the wintertime. I didn't care. I was going full steam ahead. I felt like if I was goin' ta' jail, there was no need in me stoppin', so fuck it. I would just stay strong and keep clockin', and that's what I did.

See the one thing that came outta' slavery that we learned, was how to be strong.

Man our forefathers went through hell on those boats, you know, crossin' the Atlantic, sleepin' in their own filth, then enduring all that bullshit throughout slavery. So now, those of us who are decendants of that misery, are strong. We're bitter and strong and able to withstand all kinds of pressure that otherwise the average human would not be able to stand.

Plus, we were created by God to deal with great pressure, thus makin' us even stronger. Just look at our hair. Even our hair is stronger than everybody elses. It has strength. It stands straight up instead of lyin' down like everybody else's.

You gotta give it to the white man though for usin' his genius to break us down and tryin' to create the illusion that we are weak, but they were only able to do that because they had the marketin' tools to create that illusion. Like how they created pool and made it where the object of the game is to take the white pool ball and once you take the white pool ball and shoot the black one in the whole, the game is over.

I could give you a million subliminal messages of how they try to break us down from our natural leadership roles. But for many of us we know how to look past all the hundreds of negative messages meant to keep us weak and in submission. And I was one of the one's that overlooked that trickery. I may have been wrong for what I was doin', but I was still standin' on the strength of my natural heritage and I wasn't budgin' for shit.

Plus the way I really felt about it was that everybody else in America had done what the fuck they'd wanted to do. The Kennedy's and everybody else had done their dirt and then infiltrated into the main stream. The government was always creatin' some illegal shit. Like Agent Orange, which left all them soldiers fucked up. Even na', a lot of those guys that went to Desert Storm are comin' back here havin' babies with no face, no arms, and no legs 'cause some illegal chemical they done created just so they can come out on top. So if they could do what they wanted to do I felt like why couldn't I. You may not want to give me credit for doin' the same thangs that they do to get over, but fuck it. I don't need credit. I did what I had ta' do and I was the best at it.

Throughout the months, things continued to go well. I was saving ten thousand dollars a day, so I felt pretty good about that. I also always felt that no matter what, I should always have money so whenever one of the crew would catch a case, I could send my man W. Otis Culpepper to represent them.

I'd met Culpepper in 1978 when he was still in the public defender's office. When I met him I knew right off that he was somebody special. The man was young, tough, and he knew the law. Everytime he went in to represent one of the Young Boys, he was doing an excellent job of gettin' the person off. So, I told Culpepper to come on outta' the public defenders office and get his own office and work for himself. He was too good to be practicin' law at that level. He also had a friend name Bud and Bud was giving him the same advice, so Culpepper resigned from the public defenders office and went on and started his own law practice. Culpepper would go on to become one of the biggest criminal attorneys in the city.

After Otis went into private practice, me, Otis, and Block became really tight. Me and Block had bought this big hundred and fifty thousand dollar house out in Farmington Hills which we'd purchased in Block's girlfriend T.J. and my wife's name. Anyway, the three of us had become so close that Block turned the house over to Otis and let him live there. But some kinda' way Block ended up cheatin' Otis out some money and their friendship kinda' fell apart.

Block, who didn't much care about gettin' along with anybody, then ended up gettin' into it with Baby Ray. They got into it over T.J. after Baby Ray started fuckin' her. I believe Block was fuckin' her first, then Baby Ray ended up fuckin' her and Block found out about it. This wasn't the first time this had happened. Either Baby Ray had a girl and Block would start fuckin' her or Block would have a girl and Baby Ray would start fuckin' her. So, those two had a personal thang going but because they were both like brothers to me, I stayed out of their battles.

Even after Baby Ray shot Block as a result of all of this, I still stayed out of it.

Speaking on gettin' shot, that was the third time that Block had been shot. The first time he got shot was in the shoulder when someone tried to stick us up and Block took the gun from 'em. After Block had taken the gun we fucked the mothafuckas up and took our money back. But like I said Block got shot in the process.

The second time Block got shot, a guy named William L. shot him about the same thang Baby Ray shot him for. He had tried to fuck his wife or woman, or somethin' like that and, William took it to him.

The third time, I guess he couldn't take it. I guess he couldn't fade Baby Ray, because he felt like all the guys was gone line up against him behind Baby Ray. I don't know what it was, he never talked to me about it and I never took sides one way or the other. Anyway Block ended up leavin' town, and that put an end to that. So that just left me, Baby Ray and W.W. to hold it down.

After Block left town W.W. got a cocaine connection, and started sellin' cane. He got a guy named Quinton to help him and they started boomin'. W.W. started makin' thousands a day from that stuff. Plus he started backing concert promotions. But even after that he still wasn't satisfied. After he married this girl named Dorothy she put him up on a heroin connect outta' California and he began to sell both heroin and cocaine. Baby Ray who wasn't much on organizing didn't do much in the way of rollin' after he opened his own house. But more on W.W. and Baby-Ray a lil' later.

At that particular time, they were callin' me The Guy. I didn't name myself that my cousin Kethon a.k.a., The Terrible did. I was the guy that made thangs happen. If they had a problem, I was the one that helped them solve it. If they needed or wanted somethin', I made it happen for 'em. It was as simple as that.

I found out at an early age that if you got money, then you have power. Anythang was possible with money. I had Culpepper on my side and as far as I was concerned we were the dream team. I had money, and he had influence, character, and knowledge. I basically stayed on my square, because I don't smoke, drink or get high. It was the same way with Timmie (Slim) Peoples. And to add a plus to his character-he was also non-violent. I wasn't, so I'd send Slim to places where I wouldn't be comfortable to handle certain situations.

Plus, people preferred to deal with Slim over me. Slim was more people oriented, real easy to talk to. He was a real nice guy, a real nice person to get along with. When I bought my house in Oak Park, I bought him a house too. I loved him like a brother. I still love him like a brother to this day. I'll always have some love for him. I also bought Betty a house out in Lathrup Village while I was at it.

Also while I'm on the subject of givin' love, I wanna' let my man Kirk McGurk know that I'm still down with you bro'. Don't let nobody tell you different. Hold your own while you're in the joint, and don't let nobody pull nothin over on you, 'cause you a lot smarter than what people think. So be strong and much love to you bro'.

Right around the time that I bought the houses, Culpepper was callin' me everyday tellin' me I was goin' to jail. He was tryin' to give me some nice, sound advice, but I didn't want to hear it 'cause I'm an Aries-I'm hard headed. I was only interested in doing my own thang. I was livin' a dream. I felt like at that particular time, fuck the government. I'm down like four flat tires. They either gotta' put me in jail or put me in hell. I wasn't gone stop unless they did just that.

Their first move came one day as I was drivin' down the street and the feds pulled me over and took me back to my house out in Oak Park. They had already pulled Portia over in the Vette so she was at the house when I got there. She wasn't in the house she was outside in the car.

Even though they had a warrant, I didn't feel like I should have to cooperate with 'em. I felt like why should I have to open the door. But it didn't matter, if I didn't open the door they were gonna' kick it down so I went on and opened it. I had nothin' in the house anyway, 'cause it was my golden rule not to keep anything where I laid my head. But I was trippin' on how they'd found out where I lived 'cause I was real secretive about that.

I later found out that my so called friend, Fat Prat, who lived down in the Brewster Projects had told them. Prat had ended up catchin' a case down in the Brewsters; but all the fool had to do was come to me and I would have gotten him out of whatever it was he was caught up in.

See that's what I was sayin' about everybody havin' the balls to be in the game. This guy had more faith in the white man than he had in me and the dynasty we had all built. Rather than deal with his problems like a true blue, he was more willing to sing like a bird and fly away from the rest of the flock and turn on us. This attitude was another thing that the white man had taught us.

What happened was, back in slavery the slave owners had been advised that the best way to succeed with us was to separate the light skinned from the dark skinned, and the old from the young, and the women from the men. And then to break them down to the point where if you asked one to tell on the other, there would be no half steppin'. They would bust on you in a minute and that's one of the genius things that the white man came up with to continue to rule us.

That's why Fat Prat felt it necessary to go rat on me because I guess it was still in his blood to be weak and fall for that slave shit 'cause that's exactly what that fool did.

Anyway the feds stepped on in the house and ushered me and Portia into my little daughter's pink and white dream room. Everything in it was pink and white and I had bought her everything imaginable that you could buy a little girl. My kids weren't home at the time, the only people there was me, Portia, an IRS agent, two or three D.E.A agents, an A.T.F. agent and this guy named Gerald Benacki-the D.E.A. agent I told you about earlier.

He came in and was like, "We finally got you Butch. I finally got with some people that's gonna' take you down.

But I didn't give a fuck about what he was sayin', because I had did a bit up at the Hill already and the Hill is considered one of the hardest prisons in the country. So I was like fuck it. You ain't got nothin' that I can't handle so get the fuck outta' my face and stop tryna' scare me. Either put up or shut up. That's the way I felt abou

Plus I'd already been picked up over fifty times on different charges and they had yet to prove anything. So the rhetoric he was blowin' about me bein' in trouble went in one ear and out the other.

Anyway, they had me and Portia held up in the room from about 6:00 p.m. when they flagged us to about 8:00 p.m. Every fifteen minutes or so they'd come back in the room and ask me and Portia what we had in the house; like we were gonna' help them with their search.

As far as I was concerned they was just wastin' a lot of our time. Talkin' that "This is the federal government shit, and you ain't dealin' with the Detroit Police" like it actually made a difference. Man that shit was going in one ear and out the other. I was making more money than the President so who the fuck did they think they were scarin'.

Can you just imagine the mindset I had at that particular time. I'm tellin' you, I can truly relate to the way Al Capone and all those other true gangsters felt.

I too felt like I could not be touched.

While they were searchin' the house, the only thing I could think about, was what in the hell was takin' them so long to search it. But come to find out what they were really doin' was not searchin' the house at all. They were tappin' it.

They put live taps in my living room, my bedroom, my kitchen, and my basement. The only room they didn't put taps in was the one we were held up in.

After they finished their so called search of the house they didn't get nothin' but about three hundred singles and some snapshots. I was gone send the snapshots to my friend D.J. who lived down south. It was about fifty pictures of the cars I had an' stuff like that. They still got the pictures today.

Also, while the feds were executin' the search warrant on my house, they were also executin' another on Tracey Street, which was one of S Man's houses. They ran in on him and ended up taking eight hundred thousand dollars in cash from him. But the government ended up only claimin' they took six hundred and thirty-three thousand.

After that time, S got real paranoid, 'cause he's the kinda' guy that feels like he does everythang right. But in the drug game he was doin' everythang wrong. He was talkin' on the phone, tellin' everybody all his business. And on top of that, his woman, was a crack head, and a hoe. The woman was fuckin' everybody. That's how he got his connection in California. She was fuckin' him.

Felix the Cat was his name. Felix later ended up gettin' killed, but before he did I gotta' admit, he did put us down with some strong straight up raw.

Felix was sendin' S Man about ten kilos of heroin at a time. S was puttin' it down, but everytime he'd attempt to send Felix back his money, the feds would bust 'em. They would bust 'em in the airports, here in Detroit, in cars. Man they were gettin' busted all the time. Like I said, the reason why was because everytime S would make a decision he would talk on the phone about it, or tell his wife and she would get on the phone and tell whoever she was fuckin'. And of course their phones were tapped.

NEWS PHOTO / EDWIN C. LOMARDO

Investigators look over money and weapons siezed in Wednesday's drug raid.

3 safes in home

Drug bust nets $633,000

By Jim Tittsworth
News Staff Writer

Three safes, stuffed with $633,000 in cash and Young Boys Inc.-style diamond-gold jewelry, were seized in a raid on a suspected narcotics house in northwest Detroit

No drugs were discovered and there was no one in the house at the time of Wednesday's raid, the second in a month by Detroit police and U.S. Drug Enforcement Administration (DEA) officers.

The first was a May 18 raid on two apartments in the Jeffersonian Apartments on the Detroit River that netted more than $2 million in heroin and cocaine and $800,000 in cash.

The raids are the result of a yearlong investigation by police and DEA agents, said Robert DeFauw, DEA's Detroit chief. He said other raids and arrests are expected soon.

"In the past 30 days, we've hit them (the suppliers) pretty hard," DeFauw said. "Stripping them of money will cripple the tightly knit organization of suppliers, because without money, they are unable to resupply themselves."

DeFauw would not comment on who owns the house in the 18000 block of Tracey. But sources said the owner is at least a supplier of heroin to Young Boys Inc., the heroin ring that uses teen-aged boys as pushers.

In the Wednesday raid, officers, executing a federal search warrant, forced open the doors of the house and found the cash in the three safes. Another safe, anchored in cement in the basement, was empty.

DeFauw said the house was used as a "stash house," or depository, for money from street sales of drugs until the cash could be "laundered" — exchanged for bills of larger denominations.

Most bills found were $1s, $5s, $10s and $20s.

Once officers found the money, DeFauw said he would have been surprised if drugs also had been uncovered.

"In sophisticated (drug) networks, you rarely find money and drugs in the same place," he said. "They keep them separate in case one place gets hit."

I hate to say this but S Man's wife didn't have no respect for him, nor does she have any morals, principles, or respect for herself. She was just a low down slut, bitch. S Man's family tried to talk sense into him about her but like some people in love, he just wouldn't listen.

One day, S Man came over to the house I shared with Betty over on Archdale and while he was there he used the phone. At that particular time, the feds had this tracer called trapped trace. If you called a number and that number was tapped, it would automatically trap the number you was callin' from. It would give the feds a chance to get the name the phone was in, and the address. Once they got the address they would surveillance the house.

Now right after S used the phone this guy got busted with a hundred and five thousand dollars at the airport and his slut wife started complain' about how they were gone explain the shit to Felix.

But what really came outta' all of that was the feds picked up on where I was on a daily basis and they started layin' outside my crib. It didn't take them long after that to figure out that me and S were doing business.

S was really cool with me, but he did a lot of destructive things that I truly did not agree with. Like the time he talked to a federal agent over the phone about his taxes. I knew he was talkin' to somebody about them but I thought he was talkin' to a tax attorney. But one day S said, "Yeah big boy, I been talkin' to this federal agent on the phone, tryna' get my taxes together." I said, "Man, is you crazy? What is you doin', that's what attorneys are for. They yo' mouthpiece. You done made a crucial mistake." He had let that good cop, bad cop thing get him trapped.

I remember when they came to my house, the agents were sayin' that whatever they found at S's spot on Tracey Street they were gone pin on me. They thought I was a cherry or rookie who didn't know that they couldn't pin nothin' regarding him on me. They weren't judges or nothin', they were just D.E.A. agents as far as I was concerned.

I was just listenin' to the agents play good agent/ bad agent, They take those psychology classes during their trainin' and they think they can run that shit on everybody. But everybody ain't stupid.

But they had S going. They told him that I had taken narcotics to the Tracey Street location and the reason they had executed the warrant was because of me.

But the truth is the way that they'd known about Tracey was because they had tapped his phone and he and his wife had pretty much told the Fed's where he was. I had already knew how they had found my house. They found my house from Prat. I wasn't even sweatin' it, 'cause like I said, there wasn't anythang in my house, but some dollar bills, and some pictures. Anyway after they played the good agent bad agent thing on S Man, I guess he just concluded that I had told them where he was and that was that. He ended up tellin' the "Good agent" all his business.

As a matter of fact, that's how the federal government began dealin' face to face with S. He had been dealin' with this guy named John Thomas and Thomas had unknowingly started doin' business with the government. Well, John Thomas introduced S to his "Government connect", S pushed Thomas out of the picture and now S was dealin' directly with the government himself.

Everybody knows that you don't do business with people that you don't know. Not hand ta' hand. But S bein' greedy, felt like he was gone cut the middle man out, which was John Thomas. He was gone deal with the guy himself, not knowin' that the guy was an agent. He called himself circumventin' around John Thomas. That's how the D.E.A. was playin' it. They wanted to meet the big man and as it turned out, they did.

I'm tellin' you, S did a lot of things out of greed. At one point he was sellin' me raw and sellin' the same thang to Pony Down, my competition. I remember one time I said to him, "Man, those guys got some dope that's just as strong as mine." And he was like, "Don't worry Big Boy, you just keep doin' what you doin'."

I'm tellin' you, the man was greedy. Greed should be in the dictionary with his picture right there, and on the next page should be stupid with his picture right under it.

I know when S reads this book he's gone be burnin' up, but I don't give a fuck! I don't give a fuck who don't

Corporate know-how built Young Boys

By Don Ball
News Staff Writer

It was a lot like any other well-run, successful business.

This organization had worldwide connections for its merchandise, boasted of a fluid, assembly-line production system, an extensive and efficient distribution network and even had to deal with frustrating government regulations.

That's the "corporate" profile that emerges from confidential investigative reports and other transcripts of Young Boys Inc., a $350,000-a-week heroin and cocaine drug-trafficking operation that flourished in Detroit for six years.

A two-year investigation by undercover agents from the U.S. Drug Enforcement Administration (DEA) and the Detroit Police, aimed at dismantling the organization "from the top," led to federal indictments Dec. 7 against 41 persons suspected of being connected with the drug ring.

The main person arrested was Sylvester "Seal" Murray, 30, of Southfield, reputed to be the chief supplier of narcotics for the organization. Another key figure indicted in the crackdown was Milton "Butch" Jones, 28, of Royal Oak, said to be a chief executive of Young Boys Inc. The other 39 indictments were against persons charged with assisting Jones and Murray in the transportation of drugs, arranging sales and taking drug orders over the telephone.

After the indictments, confidential investigative reports, affidavits and wiretap trancripts became public in Federal Court, and provide the following insights into the workings of the drug ring.

★ ★ ★

Although police and federal agents confiscated $700,000 in cash in a raid on a Young Boys counting house in the Jeffersonian Apartments and $600,000 from a house on Tracey street, there was no appreciable slump in its street sales of heroin and cocaine.

After the Jeffersonian raid in May, wiretap transcripts show Young Boys' alleged main supplier of narcotics, Sylvester Murray, was badly shaken. He told a friend it was "doom night." Then came the next blow, on Tracey.

But a month after the Tracey street raid, an affidavit alleges, Murray had another $200,000 in cash which he sent with two couriers on a buying trip to the West Coast, where they were arrested. Agents confiscated the couriers' cash, too.

But still, there was no dent put in Young Boys' operation. That didn't happen until Dec. 7.

★ ★ ★

The investigation that led to the indictments took two years, and one court affidavit registers this disappointment:

"... None of the electronic surveillances or searches have resulted in evidence or information .... showing how this large organization has been financed, nor is there any evidence in how the large proceeds are laundered."

★ ★ ★

The investigation did, however, turn up one source of the heroin that Murray reputedly sold to Young Boys and to other Detroit dope rings. One affidavit says

Continued on Page 8A

Flair for business built Young Boys

Continued from Page 3A

Murray had contacts in Jamaica with the organization of Montree Zeemakorn, whom the U.S Drug Enforcement Agency identifies as a worldwide dealer in southeast Asian heroin.

★★★

How organized was Young Boys Inc.? Very, a Detroit police informant says.

The informant explained to an officer that Young Boys employed a workforce of about 300 persons under the direction of "Butch" Jones. The informant guessed Young Boys netted about $50,000 daily from heroin sales.

He said the heroin was prepared for street sale on an assembly line at a house on Monterey street, where young men and women worked on a production line.

Some "cut" the heroin (diluting it with a mix such as quinine to cut the strength to about 1.5 percent actual heroin). Others measured the mixture in "spoon" amounts and placed them in coin envelopes. (One affadavit estimated that Young Boys bought 6,000 to 9000 coin envelopes weekly.)

Another group stamped the envelopes with a trademark (names such as "Hoochey Kan," "Whip Cracker," "P Funk," etc.) and assembled them in bundles of 10.

Runners then delivered hundreds of the bundles to two homes on Tuxedo. There, another crew would break up the shipments into allocations for specific areas: the east side, Woodrow Wilson area, the Jeffries Projects, the Brewster Projects, Beechwood area, Warren and Garland Area, Dexter area, Pontiac.

Another informant told Detroit police that sales in the Jeffries Projects were "real slow last August, only $3,000 a day."

Deliveries to the areas were made by "specific, designated cab drivers who were either paid in cash or provided heroin."

The envelopes were in the various areas no later than 9:30 a.m. They were given to those (usually juveniles) who made the actual sales to users. Supervisors of the sellers were known as "Top Dogs" or "Tops."

Sales normally stopped at 9:30 p.m. and the proceeds were sent back up the distribution ladder.

★★★

Sometimes an undercover agent's cover is not all he thinks it is.

~~One of the accused conspirators~~ is John E. Thomas, 35, of Wreford avenue, always referred to by his associates as "Jay Tee" or "Tee." He was a target for one of the undercover DEA agents on the case — and suspected as much.

In a March 26, 1982, telephone call to Murray, monitored with court approval, Thomas told about his meeting the previous day in the Michigan Inn with a man claiming to be a big dope dealer.

Thomas told Murray ... "ain't no doubt that he's the feds, I can tell you a million things that he has done that a big-time fella wouldn't do.

"He called me by my full name ... you know you wouldn't do that, people wouldn't do that. He told Sammy just straight up, 'Give John Thomas the thing.'

"This been a year and a half and he been still trying ... Don't nobody stay like that, man, nobody but the police."

★★★

Dope dealers find governmental red tape just as frustrating as legitimate businessmen.

Young boys' daily cash take usually was in $10 and $20 bills and a routine task is the conversion of the small bills into large denomination bank notes.

However, a new federal banking regulation requires "Money Transaction Form No. 4789" to be filled out and signed if the transaction involves $10,000 or more in cash. The form includes questions about the names and locations of the individual or firm making the transaction.

A court affadavit relates the dismay of a Young Boys "executive" when informed about the new requirement in early 1980. He told the bank official he would be back.

True to his word, the dealer returned two or three times monthly after that, each time exchanging from $8,000 to $9,000 in $10 and $20 bills for a like amount in $100 bills.

His final visit to the bank was last month.

like this mothafuckin' book. It's like I said, I ain't hard to find and anybody that's got a problem with this book can come and see me. There's been a many mothafuckas that done came to see me and there's been a many mothafuckas that done had chalk circled aroun' 'nem. Flat out.

After awhile I had made so much money that I started thinkin' about makin' movies. I mean, what else could a man with millions do. So I hooked up with the law firm of Bell, Hudson and Gardner to assist me. They were the most prestigious black law firm in Detroit at the time and the ex Judge, Edward Bell was the head of it.

I decided since the police were takin' so much money from everybody, you know, nine thousand here and ten thousand there, why not spread the money around. Give his law firm a little action. Plus they recovered money for us through the forfeiture law, which bascially stated; you couldn't just take a person's money when you felt like it. You had to convict first. So they recovered a lot of money for us.

Through dealin' with Bell and Hudson, I ended up meetin' Don King and Jane Kennedy. I met Jane Kennedy at a benefit for Bell given by Operation Push. While there, I also met and took pictures with Jesse Jackson.

After talkin' back and forth with Jane for awhile she gave me some scripts for some movies to finance and I looked them over .

Even at that particular time, I wanted to make movies about the streets and tell my version of how I saw this dirty game. So she gave me two or three movie scripts and out of them, I liked one.

What happened though, when she took the scripts back to California and told the executives she had somebody to finance the movie, Twentieth Century Fox and Paramount Pictures found out who I was and said no. Absolutely not. Somehow, they had found out that I was under investigation for running a continuing criminal enterprise and they didn't want anythang to do with my dirty money. So that was that.

Through Bell and Hudson, a lot of big things seemed possible, but as it turned out, money from the hood is not as easy to turn over as if you from the suburbs, you know.

One time me and a few other investors invested a quarter of a million dollars into this project that would grant the lucky winner the owner of the cable company that ended up being known as Barden Cable. The mayor, Coleman Young and Bell were pretty good friends at the time so we figured that we had a pretty good chance at winning the contract. But it wasn't to be. Coleman awarded the contract to Don Barden and I ended up losing a lot of money. That kinda' taught me about investin' in things I had no control over.

After that, I hooked up with this brilliant tax attorney named James Feaster. Through him, I invested in some IBM machines, which we leased out to Ford

Motor Company. I made some pretty good money off that investment. Then I also invested in a bunch of tractors and some other things. Basically, the whole reason for hookin' up with him was to help to turn my money legit.

But mind you, in no way shape or form was I ready to get out the dope game. The money I was makin' was much too much and the heroin much too strong. So I wasn't about to give that up.

I was the king of heroin sales in Detroit, and probably the country and I had every intention of keepin' it that way.

During this time I was gettin' heroin called China Four. It was the strongest heroin in the world. It had a morphine base. From this particular kinda' China white, you could take one ounce and make twenty ounces of mixed jive. Basically, if you spent a thousand dollars yo' profit was gonna' be ten thousand. This was the kinda' profit that was bein' made off this particular heroin.

With my blow Check Mate, which was also sellin' real good, I went and got a stamp made with a horse's head on it. I was really tellin' the government that I'd won. 'Cause I felt like regardless of whatever happened, I was sittin' on five million dollars and so I had to be considered the victor. Man I began to feel like I was the richest man in the world. Five million dollars!

One thang for sure, after everything that S Man had gone through I had gotten somewhat paranoid about gettin' my money taken, so I took great measure to make sure that my money was so spread out that the government couldn't get their hands on it if they wanted to. I had money hidden in my house in Troy, I had about two million hidden in the house in Highland Park, the cops never even went over there, I had money over one of my aunts house, money in safes at my mother's house, another two million in an old refrigerator over my mother-in-laws house, and money over Betty's house.

There was a difference between S's paranoia and mine though. S was blamin' everybody else for his downfall. Let him tell it, everybody was tellin' on him. Everybody else was doin' thangs wrong. But you well know by now he was the one tellin' all his business on the phone and he was the one that started dealin' with this guy named John T. who was sellin' dope directly to a D.E.A. undercover agent. And he was the one who cut out John T., out of greed and started dealin' hand to hand with the D.E.A. undercover agent himself.

Anyway, with the heroin we were sellin', if you used it for two or three days with no mix, you would have a habit. Check Mate and Hoochie Con was really habit formin'.

To show you how strong the heroin was, I had to put a limit on it of only two packs at a time, because if you took more than two packs chances was that you was gonna O.D. That's basically what it boiled down to.

Unfortunately, people would fen' so bad for the shit that after they'd gone over their limit, they would go behind our backs and send somebody else in to buy two more packs. They would shoot two or three more packs, go into convulsions and O.D. and die. Foam and shit would be droolin' all outta' they mouth and they eyes would be stuck up in the back of their heads and when the E.M.S. came ta' take 'em away, well all I can do is shake my head at the sight.

But that's the stuff that was goin' on back then, ya' know. You couldn't do nothin' about it 'cause that was the way they wanted it and if that's the way they wanted ta' die, well I had no control over that.

48 HRS.

In a city accustomed to heroin abuse, nine deaths in two days suggests a chilling trend

By STEPHEN BRAUN
Free Press Staff Writer

The blue van rattled south on the highway, metal shuddering with every stretch of bad road, on its final run of the night.

On this night, as every night, the van was delivering the dead of Wayne County to the Medical Examiner's Office in downtown Detroit. Between 4 and 11 p.m. Dec. 2, there had been a suicide by hanging, two natural deaths and a heart attack on a golf course. Now, less than an hour before midnight, a fifth was on its way.

The driver, Wilson Hall, and his partner, Alfred Burch, technical assistants from the Medical Examiner's Office, had been summoned to Holy Cross Hospital on the city's northeast side. As always, they had forms to fill out, nurses and physicians to contact, an investigation to pursue. All of that had to be accomplished before Hall and Burch could load the body onto a collapsible stretcher and into the back of the van. Now, with only minutes remaining in their shift, they sped downtown on I-75, swapping tales about their jobs and their children, oblivious to the scenery that hurtled past.

Free Press/MARY SCHROEDER
Packets of Checkmate heroin

THE CARGO from Holy Cross was the body of a heroin addict, Case 82-8402, a woman who had nodded off into unconsciousness and death five hours earlier after injecting the drug into her thumb. To Hall and Burch, who five nights a week ferry the corporeal results of all forms of death, a dead heroin addict was nothing unusual.

But over the next 48 hours, heroin would claim eight more victims in Wayne County, and the Medical Examiner's van would take more heroin abuse victims to the county morgue at 400 E. Lafayette than it normally does in a two-week span.

Between Thursday night, Dec. 2 and Saturday night, Dec. 4, nine people with little in common except an appetite for heroin collapsed and died.

Chapter 5

Murder

By 1982 the individual spots were movin' so good, that Monterey and Dexter was takin' down twenty ta' twenty-five thousand dollars a day by itself. Nothin' under twenty-thousand. The Brewster Projects was takin' in a standard thirty-thousand a day. The Jeffrey Projects ten thousand, Woodrow Wilson, ten thousand, Martindale and Elmhurst, twenty-thousand, Warren and Bewick, five-thousand and Southwest Detroit, another five-thousand.

These spots rolled like this everyday, three hundred and sixty-five days a year.

It was just like any other business, such as Ford, or General Motors. I had an assembly line. I was rollin' so strong at that particular time, that I had three hookup crews that worked an eight hour shift and hooked up dope twenty-four hours a day. The first crew would come in the mornin' and work from about 8:00 a.m. to 4:00 p.m. The second crew would hookup at the location and work from about 4:00 p.m. 'til 12:00 a.m. The midnight crew would work from 12:00 a.m. 'til 8:00 a.m. They all had different locations to hookup in, 'cause I never wanted all our eggs in one basket. Basically what I mean by hookup is the people who put the dope in the packs.

Luckily, by us constantly moving our spots, we never had a hookup spot busted. We had a hookup ran into by the feds, though. It was on Grand River, over a party store. It had a real big sifter on display. The D.E.A. had never seen a kilo sifter that big before. You could put a whole kilo in this sifter and shake it up on the table.

It was basically eight people employed at each hookup, so there was twenty-four people employed to hookup and drop off. Anyway, the feds ran up in the spot on Grand River and Robson with this hellified sifter and swooped it up. The feds got that and a bunch of other paraphernalia. They didn't get no money, drugs, or nothing else. That was kinda' good.

After that, everythang went top secret. The way we had it set up was that one hookup didn't know where the other one was. Now, unless you really needed to know, then you didn't. The only people who knew where all the hookup spots were, was me and Slim.

There were a coupla' other guys that I forgot to mention, Lewis and One Gun. Both of them worked for Slim. Oh, I forgot to mention Eddie Spaghetti's bitch ass name. Anyway, One Gun caught a murder case and just to show you how good Culpepper was, he beat that case too.

Man, Otis was and still is a brilliant trial attorney. There are different phases to the trial attorneys out there. There are some attorneys that are good at filing briefs and motions for you. Some are good at doin' appeals, some in doin' closin' arguments, and some at cross-examining.

Otis's specialty was cross-examinin' on the witness stand. He could get a person on the witness stand and make 'em believe that their name wasn't their name. He could have a person look outside, see it was daylight and get 'em on the stand to say it was night. Otis was by far the best trial attorney I've ever run across. He can cross-examine people in a way that it's still a mystery to me today, how he can get people to tell the truth, or get 'em to lie and impeach themselves on the stand.

To show you how good Otis was, I'd ended up catchin' another case as a result of hangin' out in the streets. This time for murder. What happened was me and my boy Papa Dupree, who was sellin' ounces of cocaine was down hangin' in this poolroom on John R and Erskine.

On this particular day we was shootin' pool, just funnin' and trippin' and this guy comes in that was suppose to have met Papa somewhere to buy an ounce of cocaine. So Papa tells the guy, "The reason I didn't meet you was because the police was ridin' hot down there so as soon as we leave here, I'm gone meet you somewhere else and still let you get the cocaine."

Now, even though Papa was tryna' be cool about the whole thing, the guy felt like Papa was frontin' him off in front of his girl, who he had with him. Now this guy was a bully type and had actually beat Papa's ass before Papa had went off to jail. Now however Papa had gotten into boxin' and liftin' weights so Papa wasn't about to let this guy Tyrone, punk him out. One thang led to another, they got into an argument, and the guy tried ta' sucka' punch Papa but Papa blocked the punch and fucked my man up.

Bam, bam, bam. He slammed him, threw him down and busted my man on up.

Tyrone's girl, Phylistine who'd gone to sit in the car was witnessin' the whole thang.

Anyway, after gettin' slammed Tyrone got up drugged and walked over to the car like the whole thing was over.

So Papa turned his back and started walkin' too. You know, he didn't really want no beef with my man. Meanwhile I'm watchin' every move my man makes because that's what my instinct told me ta' do. I got an eight inch-barreled 357 in my briefcase so I'm just watchin' my man, you know. Anyway I'm standing there and I watched as Tyrone goes to the car and his girl hands him two pistols. A 9 millimeter automatic and a 45.

So, now my mind was racin', 'cause I felt like if this guy was gone shoot Papa then he was gone shoot me, too.

Tyrone already had a reputation for killin' people.

He'd killed this guy named Rags, and another guy who's name I can't think of, but I know he'd sent two people down to the morgue with tags on their toes for sure.

So as Tyrone was comin' from the car with the two pistols, I eased into my briefcase and drew on him. Tyrone's action made me react. He looked at me and I looked at him and either he was gone shoot me, or I was gone shoot him. I was thinkin' he was gone shoot me or Papa .

Then Bam! Bam! Bam! Three shots rang out and Tyrone slumped to the ground like a rag doll.

Papa who went into shock 'cause he didn't even know my man had a gun thus nor did he realize how close he was to death, ran into the poolroom, and Phylistine jumped out of the car and ran over to Tyrone.

Come to find out, the guy back at the poolroom who'd actually told us to take the stuff outside was Tyrone's brother Frank. Frank ran outside hollerin' an' shit with a shotgun and I thought for sure he was gonna' turn the gun on me and start shootin', but instead, he ran over to Tyrone's side hollerin' like a bitch "You done shot my brother, you done shot my brother". I couldn't believe it. Here somebody just shot his brother and he was out there with a shotgun cryin'.

When he did look over at me I had regained my composure. My first instinct was to blast the mothafucka', but this guy named Fancy Game who was standin' right there an' seein' what I was about to do said, " Don't kill Frank man". Why don't you get the fuck on outta' here before the police come. So after eyein' Frank for a few more seconds and seein' that he wasn't about ta' do nothin', I took my gun, put it back in my briefcase, and walked to my car along with Fancy Game.

I immediately headed down to the Brewster's and told my boys I had just put in some work and so I was gonna' send Kethon down ta' take my place for awhile.

After that I went to the house and told Portia and Kethon what had happened. Kethon who was on the run for gettin' caught by Gerald Benacki with carrying six hundred and fifty grams of raw, and had bailed out, but never went back to court, strapped up and went down to the projects. There he joined Moe Heart and the rest of the crew.

Then Kethon, Moe Heart, Dead Eye and about ten other workers went lookin' for big mouth Frank. By the way carrying six hundred and fifty grams carried an automatic life in prison if convicted.

Now the reason they went lookin' for Frank was that Tyrone had died and Frank was now supposedly lookin' for me, so I'd thought I'd help him out a bit. He was telling everybody what he was gone do to me so I thought I'd send a lil' crew to pick him up, you know.

On the same day that I put 'em in Tyrone; Stratta and Red George, the owners of the pool hall called me 'cause they knew Frank wasn't no match for me. So, outta' respect for them I went by Red George's house to see what he wanted to talk about. When I got there Red George told me that Frank wasn't gone testify and how he was nothin' but all mouth. But I told him that I wasn't gone have that boy runnin' around talkin' about what he was gone tell the police.

Well, being the person I am, tryna' be logical, I went and let George talk me into lettin' him handle Frank. So, I let everybody know to freeze up on Frank and let Red George handle it.

Sure enough though, Frank went down to homicide and told Sergeant Rice and Lieutenant Stewart everything he knew. Which wasn't much. Lieutenant Stewart is a commander now, but then he was a lieutenant over the Squad Seven. Squad Seven is a homicide section made up of officers that investigate all homicides made in connection with narcotics.

At this particular time, Lieutenant Gerald Stewart had a hard on for puttin' anythang on Butch Jones. He felt that I was responsible for a lot of homicides. In his mind, he had three targets. Me, Baby Ray and Block. Block was gone and Baby Ray was in Alabama somewhere. So, he felt like the only person left to put some of the homicides on was Butch Jones.

Anyway, Frank identified me as the shooter and

he got Tyrone's girl, Phylistine, to identify me, too. So now I had a murder warrant out against me and the police started lookin' for me now like never before. They looked high and low and it took them three months to find me.

They caught me in a house I owned over on the east side. Stewart found out where I was and he and this squad they called Shamoo ran in on me. They surrounded the house and called me out. You know how they do. I tried to hide upstairs in an attic, but they came on upstairs with flashlights and guns drawn and pulled me outta' the little hidin' space I was in. I came down with my hands up in the air.

Outta' all the times that the police had ran in on me, that was the first time that they had actually found some money. I had forty thousand dollars on my bed that I didn't have a chance to do nothin' with, and I had ten thousand in just singles. But what they didn't know was I had a million dollars stashed down in the basement.

I laugh everytime I think about it because they'd really thought they'd hit the jackpot with that lil' money they found. They was runnin' around all excited like they'd hit the jackpot. I'll never forget it.

Anyway they called the narcotic section and got a warrant to search the house. They had already searched the house, but anytime you wanted for murder they can search the house first, find what they wanna' , then call down to the prosecutors office and request a warrant for the items they've already found. That's how they do it in Detroit.

When they handcuffed me, the only person in the house with me was my six year old son Mo Mo. Like usual the police tried to pump him for information but the only information he gave them was "I don't know who stays here. You can't ask me no questions without my attorney and his name is W. Otis Culpepper." Then, he ran off the phone number to the attorney's office. This made me real proud. You shoulda' seen the expressions on them cops faces when he said that. Yep, that's my boy and I was real proud of him that day.

Anyway I called some people and they came and picked Mo Mo up and they went on and took me downtown.

When I got down to homicide, they took me to a little interrogation room on the fifth floor. The thang about Detroit homicide detectives is that they play these little mind games with you. They play the good guy and the bad guy. They always assign two or three to investigate a murder and interrogate a suspect to find out if you tellin' the truth.

A lot of people don't know their rights, and one of those rights is the right to remain silent. A lot of people don't exercise that right. The thang is that the Detroit narcotic, homicide, and gang squad respect any person who exercise those rights, 'cause a lot of people done died for us to have those rights. You don't take those rights lightly.

So, they put me in the interrogation room and after a few minutes Sergeant Rice walked in. He introduced himself and asked me if I wanted to talk about the case.

Of course my answer was, "No, I don't have nothin' to say without the presence of my attorney."

So, he left and Lieutenant Stewart came in. Now, it was time for him to run his thang. He said, "Look Butch, all you gone do is pay all this money to an attorney, he gone try to get you a plea, and you still go to jail. You might as well tell me what happened and save yourself some money. I can help you. I can go over there and get yo' case knocked down to second degree murder, and get you a plea. You would be better off."

I said, "Is that right. Well, I'm gone tell you what I told the other officer. I don't have nothin' to say, Stewart. If you have a case against me gone and present it. I'm not makin' no statement."

The worst thing you can do is make a statement in a homicide case. They'll take that same statement over to the prosecutors office and then it becomes evidence against you in court. Everythang you say can be used against you. Therefore, they write everythang down, ask you to read it, and have you sign it. So, when it comes time to put you on the stand, they don't even have to put you on the stand, they put yo' statement on the stand. That becomes evidence. If it ever goes to a jury and the jury sees the statement you made, you're guilty.

What's the since in havin' a trial? You goin' away

for life.

There are so many brothers up in the state of corrections, in Jackson, for incriminatin' themselves. Plus, they done sent their codefendants, friends, brothers, mamas, and brothers to jail.

All for makin' statements. Do not make a statement when you're in the police department or in trouble, let yo' attorney do the talkin' for you.

I didn't make any statements, so they sent me up to the ninth floor. That's where they hold all the prisoners that's been picked up from all the different precincts throughout Detroit. They hold you on the ninth floor until it's time to go to 36th District Court to get arraigned. So, I stayed on the ninth floor in this dark, pissy, nasty cell with no bed for about two days.

One thang about the ninth precinct is that they have detention officers who used to work out of the Detroit House of Corrections, DE.HO.CO. They're not police, but officers. They treat you with respect, like you're a person. They're very down to earth people. They don't assume that everybody who comes down there is guilty. They treat em' better than your typical police officer. You might have two outta' eighteen that's assholes, but that's to be expected. I ain't got nothin' but respect for the majority of the people that work on the ninth floor of 1300 Beaubien.

When I got arraigned and sent to the county, the deputies over there for the most part were also very down to earth. The guys and sisters that work over there are cool. I don't have nothin', but love and respect for 'em. Each time I went to the Wayne County Jail they didn't show me nothin' but love.

I know a lot of you "Let's get them niggas kind of people" probably have problems with us being treated with respect, but the bottom line is, that's the mothafuckin' law. Innocent until proven guilty.

After I got fingerprinted, had my picture taken, saw a doctor, and a psychologist, I was allowed to make one phone call. Then they had me to stay in quarantine until my name was processed through the computer to be assigned to a floor and a rock. A rock consisted of a ward. In the Old Jail it's eight, ten and sometimes twelve people to a rock. In the New Jail it's twenty people to a rock, 'cause it's double bunked. In this particular case, I was sent to the Old Jail. I was on 514 which was considered an annex.

Compared to what I had experienced in those first two days, the cells were cool. Plus, everybody on your rock had the same kinda' case.

In my instance of course, it was murder. The one thing that this allows you to do is compare notes with all the other guys on how to beat your murder case and who was the best lawyer for your particular case.

During this particular time, it was highly agreed upon that Charles Campbell was an excellent murder attorney. That W. Otis Culpepper was and still is an excellent trial attorney, murder attorney, narcotics attorney, and pistol attorney. And that S. Allen Early,

Steve Fishman, Sheldon Helpburn, Lester Hudson and a few others, were also very good.

A lot of your better trial attorneys eventually became Judges or are now Judges so I'm not gonna' mention too many names 'cause I don't want people ta' get the wrong impressions or interpretations about people sittin' on the bench.

The Wayne County Jail wasn't too bad. Back then, they use to let you have green money and if you had money you could live like a king. People used to gamble, win bond money and would be outta' there. I mean people would be winnin' like five an' ten thousand dollars up in that joint.

They also used to let you wear your own clothes, but then, people started havin' fights and gettin' their clothes and money taken so they cut all that shit out.

Everyday while I was in the County my friend Wilbert Rice who was an attorney used ta' come and see me. Each time he would come, he would bring me money. I would have my wife to give him one thousand dollars every week, and he would bring me two hundred at a time. I'd take the money and have the deputies to buy me pizza, cornbeef sandwiches, roastbeef sandwiches, chicken, or whatever I wanted when they would go out to buy their lunches.

With Timmie Peoples holdin' down the fort for me while I was in the County, and me livin' good, I didn't have no complaints.

It took Culpepper a couple months before he was

able to get my case reduced to second degree murder. After that, they gave me a fifty thousand dollar cash bond, and I was outta' there.

Of course I still had the case, but at least now I was mobile. I could get around. I could get back into the groove of thangs.

I was only gone a coupla' months, so hadn't much changed. And what little that did, I had my boy Buster to fill me in.

Now that I was back out, I went to see Stratta and Red George 'cause they had promised me that they'd had some control over their boy.

After I got there I asked them what they were gonna' do about this boy Frank, 'cause now they done gave me their word that he wasn't gone testify but he'd already went down there and signed a statement against me sayin' he saw me shoot his brother. I wasn't worryin' about Philistine, 'cause she had already sent word to me that for five thousand dollars she would change her statement and that she might not even come to court.

Nevertheless, I wasn't givin' that bitch a dime. As far as I was concerned I was like fuck her. If she came to court she did so at her own risk. That's the way I looked at it.

After being out for awhile I put my own defense together. I got some people that saw Tyrone go to the car and get two pistols from Phylistine . I wasn't denyin' that I shot him, I just denied the manner in which they say I shot him. I was basin' my defense on when he acted, I reacted. That was the way I wanted Culpepper to present it to the jury, 'cause I felt like I had the right to protect myself, as well as my friend.

I told Culpepper that if he won the case I would buy him a Rolls Royce.

When it came time to go to court, the narcotic section had put out the rumor that I had bought the judge.

We were to appear before Judge Craig Strong but after that rumor, he didn't want nothin' ta' do with my case. Soon the rest of the judges in Recorders Court heard the rumor and before you knew it, nobody wanted to take the case.

So, what they did was send the case over to Circuit Court. Circuit Court basically handles cases outside of Detroit. Typically white areas. So I ended up in front of a judge in Circuit Court and the trial was on.

After we got ta' Circuit Court and started the peremptory challenges, or picking of the jury, Otis began preppin' the jury. He asked everybody if they felt that if I'd acted in self-defense could they come back with a not-guilty verdict and before it was over he got every one of them to say yes.

I knew it would only be a matter of time before I would be set free.

When the trial finally started it became a real big thang because the authorities felt like they had this big drug dealer and they were finally going to stop him.

The courtroom was packed and the prosecution

was the first to put their witnesses on the stand.

Thinkin' that they would start off their account with a huge bang, they called lyin' ass Frank to the stand.

Lookin' like a man who had been programmed and ready to say anything, Frank got up their and told the courtroom how he'd put us out of the poolroom after Papa Dupree and his brother had got into an argument, and how Papa Dupree had kicked his brother's ass after they'd gotten outside. Then he said, the next thing he knew, he seen me shoot his brother.

He didn't tell the part about his brother goin' to the car and gettin' two guns or nothin'. He was actually intent on flat out lyin' on me and sendin' me ta' jail for life. I couldn't believe that puck ass mothafucka. He wasn't even out there when the shootin' happened. I think when the jury later heard the rest of the testimony and saw that Frank had lied, it became clear that they could only bring about one verdict.

I had other witnesses that testified for me. Like Burnside and Gingerbread; some old hustlers from the downtown area, Rob Purdue also testified for me.

These were people who'd actually saw what happened. They all said the same thang as Frank, except they talked about the part when Tyrone went to the car and got the two guns to shoot me and Papa. They said it was like a draw thang. I drew my guns and he had already drew his and it happened so fast that I had no other choice. I knew I was gone beat the murder case once they got up there and told the true story, 'cause what Tyrone did made me react.

I never denied that I shot Tyrone. I denied the way the prosecutor said I shot him. The jury went out and came back with a not-guilty verdict on the strength of self-defense 'cause if Tyrone never woulda' gotten them guns, then I never would have had ta' shoot him. And almost shoot his bitch ass brother.

Chapter 6

Pontiac

After I beat the murder case, sales skyrocketed. I looked up and I had fifteen different spots in Detroit. One of the guys who was responsible for the smooth operation of these spots was my man Rickey Peoples, who was no relation to Timmie and Baby Ray. His job was to work out of Ollie May's house on Monterey between Dexter and Homer and distribute heroin to the runners. Each morning, I would drop off between eighty to a hundred thousand in heroin, then between fifteen to seventeen cabs would pull up with runners ready to pick up their dope.

Some spots would get ten thousand, some seven thousand, some five thousand, and some got three thousand. Eventually, with all the activity going on outside, the police finally busted Ollie May's house and so we moved across the street to my homegirl Dee Dee's house.

Rickey didn't get caught the day they ran up in Ollie's house so he continued to pass out the bags when we moved across the street. Man we had a smooth operation. The way we would pass out the bags was that we would stamp the names of the streets each person worked on their bags.

Like Woodrow Wilson. Minute Man worked on Woodrow Wilson. Kirk was down on Lawton. We had bags for McGraw, Dexter, Martindale, Linwood, the Jeffrey Projects, the Brewsters, for John R and Erskine, Pontiac, Flint, Southwest Detroit, for Warren and Bewick, and Gratiot on the east side. Everywhere the heroin was sold we had a bag for it and somebody down there to hold down the spots.

One thang I liked about Rickey Peoples was no matter how much heroin I gave him, he knew who had what. He knew who'd dropped off money, and who didn't. He had it all in his head. He was like a mathematical genius when it came to numbers. He never forgot one number or who owed what.

Out of all the spots I had, Dexter rolled the strongest. It rolled so strong that if you were from one of the other spots and you had a bag for five thousand and you had only sold four and had ten bundles left, then you could take it to Dexter and sell it within a few hours. Matter fact, whoever didn't finish sellin' their bundles by 6:00 p.m., took their bundles on Dexter to sell the

Suspected heroin warehouse raided

Detroit police arrested two adults and seized 2,200 packets of suspected heroin during a raid Wednesday on a west side home believed to be a major distribution point for the Young Boys Inc. heroin ring.

Officer Delbert Jennings of the police narcotics section said nine officers raided the home at 3736 Monterrey at 9:30 a.m. and took a 22-year-old man and a 28-year-old woman into custody.

Jennings refused to identify them until their arraignment, scheduled in 36th (Detroit) District Court today.

Jennings estimated the stree value of the suspected heroin at $38,000. He said the packets seized were stamped "Raw Dog," "P-Funk" and "CBS" — all expressions commonly used by Young Boys members to describe types of heroin.

Police sources describe Young Boys as a well-organized ring that uses pre-teens as drug runners and maintains a fleet of expensive cars to distribute heroin. Police believe the operation nets about $400,000 a week.

The ring reportedly uses pre-teens as its runners because he children, if arrested, are not likely to be prosecuted or imprisoned.

The alleged distribution center, which reportedly handled $250,000 a week in street sales, supplied the Dexter-Richton area, Jennings said.

"We got (Wednesday morning) what we figure was the morning supply," Jennings said.

Young Boys has received a great deal of attention after the March 29 slaying of Officer William Green. Police sources said the 17-year-old accused of the slaying may be a member of the group.

remainin' stuff there. Dexter was like our strong hold. The corner of Dexter and Elmhurst

And I'm tellin' you, we didn't allow no competition on Dexter. Flat out. If you wasn't sellin' Check Mate, Dyno, Murder One, or C.B.S, all Y.B.I. blows then you'd bet not get caught sellin' dope on Dexter.

Everytime somebody had trouble at one of their spots Rickey Peoples brother, Billy, would handle it. It wasn't nothin' that he couldn't handle. If somebody was givin' me problems I'd just tell Billy and it was handled. It didn't matter who it was or what the assignment was, if Billy got it, it was as good as did.

People like him is what made the Y.B.I. so strong.

To show you how tough Billy was, I'd started datin' this girl from the Brewster Projects named Tamara. She knew everybody in the projects and basically that's how we got in. I knew a coupla' people who lived down there, like Papa Dupree and Rob Purdue but she was the one that had really hooked us up with everybody. Anyway when we got down there strong she started fuckin' me.

Her boyfriend, Crooked Mouth Mike, didn't like it so he sent back word that he was gone fuck me up, you know. When Billy heard about it, he went down there and shot my man dead in the face. No questions asked.

Now they call my man Blind Mike.

Speakin' of Rob Purdue, he was also like a brother ta' me. Everytime I would be locked up in the State joint, he would be locked up too. When I went to

Marquette, Rob was there. When I went to camp, Rob was there. Everywhere I jailed, Rob was there.

I had met him and X though Block after Block had did his first bit. X used to play basketball so strong that the Pistons came up to the jail and took him outta' Ionia. But he liked to stick-up thangs so bad that he never made it anywhere but back to prison. X was Papa Dupree's crime partner. From hangin' out in the streets, both of 'em ended up goin' back ta' jail for a murder that they didn't even commit. It was a stick-up that went bad and this guy named Hair Man got killed.

But gettin' back to Billy, all I can say is, he was my man. Me and him was like brothers, too. The thang about Billy was that he loved his work. He would dress up like a girl, put on a wig, some makeup and lipstick and head out on his mission. I guess that was his forte'. He had a natural talent for it. He just loved takin' assignments and knockin' off people.

He's dead now, but I wish he was here to see this book bein' made, 'cause I know he woulda' really loved that 'cause there was nothin' that I did that he didn't support.

I never told nobody in the Y.B.I. who was doin' dirt for me, 'cause I did thangs on the need to know basis. If it wasn't relevant to them, then they didn't need to know. I would give Billy three thousand, five thousand, and ten thousand dollar assignments. Whatever I felt the assignment was worth or whatever he asked me for. I had known Billy all his life and we'd never had an argument, that was one guy that I'll never forget.

I had so many spots, and so many people who wanted to beef with me, that other people started gettin' into the act of solving our problems.

If Farod wasn't, then Kirk was, if Kirk wasn't, then Richie Rich, Moe Heart, Kethon, Dead Eye or Minute Man were solving problems.

My crew was so down that we governed everythang we saw.

We came, we saw, and we conquered. That was our attitude and that was the way we rolled.

I always believed that there was safety in numbers. So, when we went to a spot, I might send two or three there one day, but on the next, it would be five guys workin' that spot.

We had fifteen to twenty people workin' a spot when we were down in the Brewster Projects. That was because they had the geographical thang. Nobody wanted me sellin' raw in the Brewsters, 'cause they felt like I was from Dexter, the west side, and they were from downtown. They couldn't get with that. So, everytime somebody came to me and told me I couldn't roll down in the Brewsters I would shoot him in the leg and tell him that whoever told him to come to me to take that bullet back to him.

After I shot about eight or nine people, they left me alone and I didn't have any more problem out of the Brewsters.

When you're rollin' like we were, you had no choice

but to wake up and go to bed with trouble on yo' mind. That's just how it was. Every single day I knew it was gone be somethin'. So, I felt like whoever brought me some drama I was gone take it to them and that's just the way it was.

I wasn't the type of guy that just went around startin' shit, but neither did I take any off nobody. If you started somethin' with me, I was gone finish it, and if I didn't finish it, then one of the people I mentioned would.

I felt like I was down with the best hustlers in this city. When it came to gettin' money, I wouldn't wanna' get money with anybody else, 'cause they were true to the game and the game was true to them.

One thang that we didn't play was that tellin' thang. Everybody knew that if the narcotic section, Detroit Police, or the gang squad knocked us off, then nobody would say nothin'.

Unfortunately however, we had a coupla' guys break bad.

Punk ass Lug Head was one. And all you other Lug Head mothafuckas know who you are, too. To me, you're some of the most low down, dirty, takin' it in the ass, dick suckin' mothafuckas. Let it be known if you're ever seen on the streets, people are looking for you. It's outta' my hands. You dug your own grave and now you're gonna' have to sleep in it. And I don't give a fuck.

See, them guys broke the golden rule and that's how the game goes. They sat up there and took the stand, got a lot of people indicted, and brought down a hellava' organization. I didn't twist nobody's arm to be down with me. Goin' to jail an' all that stuff was all part of the territory.

I felt like I walked the walk, 'cause I talked the talk. I backed up everythang I said. Therefore, when it came time for me to do some time, I wasn't worried about it. I always felt like, fuck 'em. I can hold mine. You had to have that kinda' attitude.

That's why I didn't let everybody roll. I didn't let everybody have a gun. It wasn't that I was tryna' make all the money, it was that I knew a lot of guys couldn't hold their mud. In other words, I knew they were goin' get in trouble and go down to the police and spill their guts. That ain't how the game goes. If you true to the game, then the game will be true to you. If you take care of yo' business, then yo' business will take care of you. That has always been my philosophy.

The money gettin' mothafucka' I am, I could see if a guy had the same qualities to hold down a spot or roll. If he didn't have no complexes, set his pride aside and was willin' to take some orders, then he could be down with me. I'd tell a guy straight up front, "All I ask is that you be loyal. Don't be no motherfuckin' rat. Just be all the way down."

See, some people are down, but the true Young Boys were all the way down. That's what made us stand out. That's why everybody across the nation, like the Crips and the Bloods, heard about how the Young Boys were puttin' it down and how they eventually woke up and saw the light. Unless you defendin' yo'self it ain't even about that gang bangin', its about clockin'. And all I gotta' say about that is clock while you can. Stack yo' loot and get out while you can. Cause once you get caught up in the system, I'm tellin' you it ain't no fun place ta' live. Just ask some of the people who locked up and can only get out an hour a day for exercise and then their back in their cells. For life.

Gettin' back to my game though, what I liked most about sellin' heroin, was that I was gettin' top grade. Like China Four. China Four heroin was a grade four, which is the strongest heroin in the world. It was comin' from Thailand plus I had heroin comin' from Bangkok, too. Basically, it was comin' from the Golden Triangles. That was what I was gettin' from S.

S had the connect and I was slangin' it.

Between him, Milwaukee Jack, and Betty like I said, I couldn't go wrong. Jack knew a bunch of people and they was slangin' it at him. The people he didn't know, my girl Betty knew. She was goin' to New York and brangin' it back as strong as it comes. And as I said before strong heroin sells itself.

It's cheaper over seas. Back then, if you put it down right, it was like one hundred percent profit. It was a lot of money to be made and everybody was just happy. The thang about my blow was that if I put it down, then it was good dope. I would only sell good dope, 'cause my name and my reputation was on the line and all the dope fiends knew that.

Now for the record, it's a difference between a dope fiend and a basehead. A basehead gets high off cocaine and a dope fiend shoots or blows heroin, 'cause he likes that heroin high. Cocaine is an upper and heroin is a downer. Heroin is a blow or narcotic for people who just wanna' sit around, nod, scratch their balls, while dribbling' at the mouth. People on that cocaine are real jittery, jumpin' up and down. They can't sit down. That's the difference. There is money in both of 'em, but ain't nothin' like sellin' that raw.

I'm a wizard at sellin' heroin, 'cause it's many tricks to the many ways you can sell it, and many forms to the different grades of heroin. You have the China White, Lebanese Heroin, Mexican Mud Heroin, Off beige heroin-which is a low-grade heroin, and then African Heroin that comes in a rock form and looks like donkey turds.

Out of all the heroin I sold, none of it came in rock forms. It came straight powder, straight clean.

China White was clean heroin. When people who would put it in their spoon, with a little water on it, it didn't take it long to cook, and when they shot it they knew they were shootin' only the best.

A coupla' guys that I'd known for awhile, Greg Fields and D.J. who'd been shootin' heroin since the sixties were my testers. They would tell me from experience how the dope held them, how it tasted, and the feelin' that it gave 'em.

I always had people to test my raw. Good twenty ta' thirty year dope fiends.

In Pontiac, Michigan, a small city not to far from Detroit, another twenty year dope fiend name Bow would be the one that would turn me on to the dope fiends in that city. I knew a few people in Pontiac already, like Baby Charles, and my good friend Pontiac Joe but Bow was a flat out dope fiend and knew all the other dope fiends in Pontiac. He used to tell me, "Man, bring that blow up to Pontiac and you can get big money." So one day I took him up on his word and went on up there and passed out some samples to see what the dope fiends would say about it. Sure enough after they tested our heroin, it was on.

I didn't have a spot in Pontiac, so I had to organize one. I took my boys Butch Rod, Bone Man, Frank D., and his brother Tyrone with us. We rented a room then went out to the park and let Bow sit on top of the sacks 'cause he knew everybody. At first Bow didn't want us to meet any of the people 'cause he wanted to get in on the money makin' aspect of the business. But we told him we wanted to meet the people that we was doin' business with, so after a few days we had met everybody and we told them that they could get the blow directly from us and so they no longer had to deal directly with Bow.

This was our game, you know. We didn't need nobody tryna' get in our way. Plus Bow loved to nod off on that Hoochie Con. The dope that we took up to

Pontiac. So how effective could he truly be?

We took the same dope up to Flint. In Flint, a lot of them guys are player haters. They don't really like guys from Detroit, 'cause they got that geographical thang. But like I said, I felt like I could go anywhere and put my blow down, and I did.

Chapter 7

The Feds

After I'd expanded our business to Pontiac and Flint there was nothin' much left for me ta' do but spend more money and have more fun. I bought about three more nice houses, about 10 more cars, and I gambled and played the numbers everyday. I would have to say that this time of my life was about the best. I'd just beat that murder case and so I actually felt as if I was indestructible. I was flying like a bird.

Of course the feds had other ideas. The more money I made, the more they pumped up their surveillance. Gerald Benacki had worked so hard that by this time he knew every single face, name, and position of every member of the Young Boy's. I still didn't really pay much attention to the feds though, 'cause I felt like,

"Fuck 'em. As long as I didn't get caught with nothin', I felt like I wasn't goin' ta' jail."

They had this one D.E.A. agent named King. He was the one who came into the house in Oak Park. I'll never forget the day he looked at me the same way that Rudy Davis had and told me, "We're gonna stop you, one way or the other." And I looked at him and asked, "What do you mean you gone stop me one way or the other?" And he said, "We gone stop you, one way or the other."

But for some reason, even though I knew he was serious, unlike Rudy Davis, this guy didn't really scare me. I don't know why, he just didn't.

Even though I wasn't thinkin' much about the government bustin' me at that time, come to find out they had somethin' on me that I wasn't quite thinkin' about. "Running A Continual Criminal Enterprise."

That's the statue under the federal code of narcotics traffickin' that they charge people who are committin' organizational crimes and makin' a substantial amount of money. But who they can't catch doin' anything red handed. They build such cases on hearsay. People tellin' on you and their observation and shit like that. I mean after you've bought so many houses and cars and done so much with money and you have no legitimate job to show for it, they do their research and that's when they come at you with the 848, or running the illegal enterprise.

Anyway, while they were tryna' put all this stuff

together to indict me I had since taken over Joy Road. Which until I took it over, was being controlled by the Chapman brothers.

How I got Joy Road, was I had a cousin named Herman Amos who'd come home from the State Joint. Before he'd gotten out, me, Kethon, Moe Heart and Dead Eye would all go up to see him about once every other month. So by the time he came home, I figured Herman would be down with us 'cause he was my cousin, and he had heart, so it was only natural that I'd expect he would be down with me.

However, when he came home, he ended up gettin' down with the Chapman brothers, who were my enemies. I didn't even know he knew the Chapman brothers. So I figured that maybe after he found out what was up, that he would come to his senses and come roll with us. But when I ended up runnin' into him, he told me he would be down with whoever the fuck he wanted to be down with, and that he had no intention of bein' down with me. You know talkin' real greasy.

I couldn't believe that this was the same guy that we had supported all while he was in prison. Plus like I said he was my cousin. I mean, what the fuck?

So, seein' that he had a nine millimeter and that he was a lil' drunk I said alright, that's cool. So I shook his hand and went on about my business.

As I walked away though I was pissed. I couldn't believe he had talked ta' me that way. I was thinkin' to myself, alright nigga' I'll catch you on the rebound.

About two or three days later Baby Ray got shot. It turned out that this guy named Kirk Alert had shot Baby Ray over some bullshittin' spot. So we all got mad and strapped up. Even though Baby Ray wasn't workin' with us at the time, he was still considered a Young Boy. So about three or four car loads of us rode on down to Highland Park to look for Kirk Alert.

As we were ridin' around we ran into Kirk's boy Fat Herbie. He and Kirk was like brothers, so I asked Fat Herbie to tell me where his boy was, so we could handle our business. So Herbie took us over on Glynn where he figured Kirk would be. It wasn't as if Herbie had much choice but to take us, 'cause he had a gang of niggas that was gone take it out on him if he hadn't. But I liked Fat Herbie and knowin' he didn't have nothin' to do with it, I wasn't gone really let anything happen to him.

Anyway, after not findin' him on Glynn, we rode all that day lookin' for Kirk with no luck. Finally we just gave up and rode back to Monterey. Man it wasn't fifteen minutes after we got over there that somebody said, "Here comes Herman Amos."

So, I said "Is that right, Somebody hand me a heater." So either Cromer or Richie Rich handed me a pistol, I dont' quite remember which.

I was already pissed about not findin' Kirk Alert so there was no better time for Herman to walk into my awaitin' arms. So, he came on down the street and when he got up to where the whole crew was standin' I asked him, "What was up with all that shit you was blowin' outta' yo' mouth the other day when I was tryna' talk some sense into you?"

Plus, Richie Rich had told me he'd come to his house and had tried to take him out, but he'd somehow got away. So, I was really heated up.

Anyway I told Herman "Talk slick na', you know. You sat up there with that mothafuckin' pistol and confronted me about those punk ass Chapman brothers, blow that shit outta' yo' mouth na'.

He could see I had fire in my eyes and I wasn't tryna' hear nothin'.

So I said again, "Say that mothafuckin' shit na', nigga! You sat up there talkin' smart the other mothafuckin' day when you had that pistol on you. Talk smart na'! Talk smart now," I said!

Na', the mothafucka started mumblin' some shit about what he didn't mean and what he hadn't said and just because he started talkin' that shit I just off and shot 'him in the leg.

It was my original plan to just pistol whip him, ya' know, but thangs didn't end up happenin' that way 'cause soon as I shot him, everybody else just started blastin' my man like the long riders. He was jumpin' and turnin' and fallin' all at the same time. He had so many bullets comin' at him that his body didn't know which way ta' go. I didn't really want him did like that, but I really couldn't say nothin', 'cause them boys was hot and once they started shootin', that was it.

After the shooting, a couple of the fellas threw Herman in the trunk of one of the cars and they dumped the body somewhere over in some alley.

Now, I was like goddamned, I gotta' go tell my mama that my cousin done got killed. Then the next day my Aunt Katherine and my Uncle Herman found out that he was dead after Heman's body was found by the police. My aunt and uncle called my mama boo-hooin' and everythang, talkin' 'bout they didn't have no money to bury him so I gave my mama two thousand dollars to give to my Aunt Katherine to bury Herman. I didn't go to the funeral 'cause I was like fuck 'em, 'I felt like the nigga' had brought his death on himself so what the fuck.

Somehow, the police told my Aunt Katherine that he got killed, 'cause he didn't wanna' join my drug organization. She didn't even know I was down with the Young Boys.

It wasn't the case, though. I don't know how they got that story. I think it was one of them Chapman brothers, feelin' like I wanted Herman to be down with me or he couldn't be down with nobody. It wasn't like that, though. It was about the disrespect thang. Like I said, people gotta' be careful about what they say, 'cause certain people you just can't be runnin' around disrespecting. I felt like he was blowin' all that James Cagney shit outta' his mouth and basically as it turned out, he couldn't back it up.

After the Herman incident nothin' much changed.

The police didn't even come that night. We picked the shells up, cleaned up, and waited for the police to show up. But they never showed up. After that I didn't even hear no more about the Chapman brothers and so we went on and took over Joy Road.

By this time, Kirk McGurk had Lawton over there boomin'! We were rollin' like nollin'! Everythang was goin' picture perfect and I couldn't have asked for better days. Then one day Kirk comes in and tells me, "W.W. came up to the spot passin' out blows tryna' take over our shit." Kirk said he told him he couldn't do that and had he asked The Guy and W.W. said, "Naw, he hadn't talked to The Guy and Fuck the Guy."

So, I said, "Man, he said that?" Kirk said, "Man, I was so hot that I wanted to blow his shit out right there, but I didn't want you to be mad at me for makin' the spot hot."

So, I said, "Kirk, you're sure that he said all that?" Kirk said, "I swear on my mama and hope she dies. W.W. said, "I ain't gotta' ask the Guy. Fuck the Guy. I can put my mothafuckin' blow down wherever I want it."

I was like, "What goddamn, mothafuckin' blow had this guy stickin' his chest out like that." Me and W. was supposed to be tight. I'd never said nothin' disrespectful to him. He had his territory and I had mine.

So anyway the next thang I know somebody done tried ta' kill my boy Chip while up on eight mile rollin' with my crew. Come ta' find out, W.W. done shot 'em.

Drug figures cleared of a slaying count

BY JOE SWICKARD
Free Press Staff Writer

Murder charges from 1982 against the founder of Young Boys Inc. and one of his alleged top enforcers were dismissed Thursday by Recorder's Court Judge George Crockett III, who ruled the prosecution waited too long to bring the charges.

However, Crockett also ruled that Young Boys founder Milton (Butch) Jones must still face trial on another 1982 killing.

Curt (Kirk McGurk) Napier, once labeled by the Wayne County Prosecutor's Office as Detroit's Public Enemy No. 1 as an enforcer, smiled and flashed a thumbs-up sign to his mother after Crockett dismissed the first-degree murder charge.

Jones grinned as he said: "One down and one to go. And I'm not guilty of anything."

Attorneys for Napier, serving a 20-to-40-year assault sentence, and Jones, serving a 12-year federal drug sentence, argued that the prosecution waited too long by not charging them until 1988 with the 1982 killing of Dwayne Davis. CASE.

The key prosecution witness, the attorneys argued, has been available since 1985.

The attorneys, Jeffrey Collins and Wallace Capel, said that witnesses who could have helped their clients are no longer available.

While granting the defense motion on the Davis slaying, Crockett refused to dismiss the case against Jones in the 1982 killing of Herman Amos.

The next thang I knew September 28 rolled around and I got a phone call. I remember the date 'cause it was Portia's birthdate, and I was plannin' on takin' her to Kyoto's, Japanese restaurant in Troy. But before we could take off my pager started goin' off like crazy. I'd say it was about 2:00 or 3:00 in the afternoon. Somebody was blowin' my pager up. They had put 911 and my mother's address on the pager so I called over there to see what had happened. The news was that W. W. had gotten killed.

I was like, "What!" They said he was over there on Lawton and somebody killed him. I then called over on Martindale to talk to Raymond and Baby Ray said, "Yeah man, I went up there to see it for myself and W. was stretched out with two ta' 'da head."

It turns out that somebody had walked up to W. and had given him a hand shake and a smile. I was like, "Is that right?!" They was like, "Yeah!"

Where I come from, a hand shake and a smile is like a death kiss.

I don't know what happened or nothin' like that. All I know is me, Kirk, Moe Heart, and Terrible ended up gettin' implicated in the murder. The police picked us up but then they let us go because we all had legitimate alibis.

Plus they didn't have any eyewitnesses.

I know I was at home with my wife when it happened. I didn't have nothin' to do with it and that's the truth.

The dope on Young Boys

You can't leave–alive

"You people who drive on the John Lodge and go past the Jeffries don't know what it's like to go hungry or see your momma tryin' to scrape to keep the family together.

"I know its wrong and illegal. But I got started 'cause I wanted to put more food on the table for my family.

"Man, they were real tight. They said I either was going to have to leave or provide. And since I ain't got much education, this was the only way. And the money is good.

"We each are makin' about $1,200 per week. It's big money, but it ain't big money by the time we pay the lawyers, we pay the judges, we pay the parents. We only getting to keep about $400 to $500.

"You got to understand that we're young. And when you're young, you don't know what to do with it. We just blow it. I know people out there who made the money and are livin' good. Some own discos, carwashes, motels ... hell, man, it's a trip. Young Boys Inc. legitimate?"

★ ★ ★

"WORKING WITH Young Boys, man, is a hard life. Man, it's a hell of a life. You can never leave. Once you know a person is organization, he's not just going to turn up and leave, and say 'I quit.' Yeah, you quit and as you walk to the door, the man goes BANG, BANG, BANG, BANG. You don't have to quit — you be gone.

"Even though I know how dangerous this is, none of us never regret it.

"There's a lot of discipline in selling dope for the Young Boys. What you've got is a business. A big business with a lot of money. And the man don' like nobody screwing up.

"Right now the thing on the streets is real tight. There's not much dope out there, and

Continued on Page 16B

Over the BRIDGE

Tomorrow, The Detroit News begins *Over the Bridge*, a five-part photo series on the Jeffries Housing Project, one of Detroit's most notorious neighborhoods. The title refers to a walkway over the Lodge Freeway that the residents use to enter or leave the world of the Jeffries.

This article is from interviews Detroit News photographer David Kryszak obtained while producing the series.

The speakers are members of Young Boys Inc., a network of youths selling packets of heroin under labels such as "Gucci Down," "Whip Cracker" and "Renegade" in the projects.

Because the wide-open drug traffic affects all the residents in some way, the series begins with the dealers and their victims.

Over the Bridge will offer a glimpse inside the Jeffries and give a voice to the people who live there. The addict, the children, the welfare mother, the white minister will all speak for themselves.

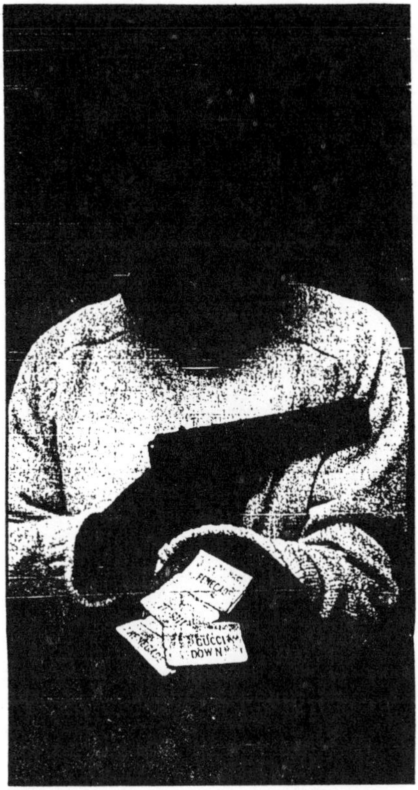

NEWS PHOTO / DAVID KRYSZAK

Wearing a hood, a member of Young Boys Inc. shows packs of heroin.

Goal: Smash street drug gangs

Police say they see results

'We are going to continue arresting members of that organization until we dismantle it.'

— Deputy Police Chief Gerald Hale, commenting on the Young Boys Inc. gang, Aug. 25, 1979

By Gene Schabath
News Staff Writer

Young Boys Inc., the openly defiant drug trafficking network that turned some Detroit streets into dangerous avenues of crime and terror, is far from dismantled.

But Detroit police claim they have made inroads on Young Boys Inc. (YBI) since Deputy Chief Gerald Hale pledged to dismantle the drug network three years ago. The organization has been weakened by a loss of some of its heroin sources and the seizure by federal agents of more than $1.4 million in cash and jewelry, police say.

The seizures, according to police, are evidence that a relentless investigation of the well-run organization by Detroit and federal narcotics agents is starting to pay off.

THE GOAL is to ferret out those at the top of Young Boys Inc. and to dismantle the organization from within.

Until now, the Young Boys hierarchy has been well-insulated from arrests by the structure of the gang, which uses juveniles as drug runners and street salesmen.

But earlier this year, federal agents teamed with Detroit police in what one agent called an

Continued on Page 16B

16-B THE DETROIT NEWS Sunday, Nov. 14, 1982

Police zero in on Young Boys Inc.

Continued from Page 1B

"all out" campaign to snuff out Young Boys. The federal grand jury also reportedly is trying to indict the financial backers of the organization.

"We're that close," said Inspector Ray Murray, commander of the Detroit Police narcotics bureau, holding his thumb and forefinger two inches apart.

"Their structure has not been broken down," Murray acknowledged. "You can bust street runners all day long and not do a thing.

"THAT'S WHY we're trying to make cases on the right people. We've made an awful lot of arrests in that organization in eight years, but we have to get to those at the top."

The inspector said the concerted federal-local crusade against Young Boys was not prompted by the March 28 killing of gang squad officer William Green by a Young Boys membr.

Green was slain and his partner, Eric Byers, critically wounded when they stopped to question a group of teens on Woodward and Leicester about Young Boys activities in the area.

Cary Vincent Goins, 17, reportedly a lieutenant in the ring, was convicted Thursday of involuntary manslaughter in the shooting death of Officer Green.

"We were working on Young Boys when the officer got killed," Murray said. "And we're still working on it. An investigation of this type can't be completed in a couple of months. We made 6,000 drug arrests last year but there's so much profit to be made it keeps going on."

SEVERAL MAJOR raids in the past five months put a crimp in the money supply used to purchase large quantities of heroin imported into Michigan. The two raids netted agents about $1.4 million in cash and jewelry and $2 million in heroin and cocaine.

"The activities (of Young Boys, Inc) are no longer as great or expansive as they once were," said Robert DeFauw, chief of the U.S. Drug Enforcement Administration in Detroit.

"We know they lost the source of their supplies and this caused them to seek out other sources," DeFauw said.

Members of the drug gang scoff at police claims that the organization has been weakened by the relentless investigation, explaining that drug activity has been curtailed because the heroin supply is low and because some drug dealers now work out of motels. But gang members claim a new shipment of high grade heroin is due to arrive in Detroit next month.

DEFAUW RESPONDED: "Oh, they can find another supplier if they shop around long enough. But they have to pay cash. They can't buy it on consignment."

Police officials also scoff at reports of territorial wars between drug dealers, but several "organizers" of Young Boys who now 'compete' in the lucrative drug trade have been shot — one fatally — in the last two months.

The latest victim was Dwayne Davis, 26, who was gunned down at midday Sept. 28 on Lawton and Columbus in the 10th (Livernois) precinct. The area, bounded by Livernois, Davison, Collingwood and the Lodge Freeway, is where Young Boys started operating in the mid-1970s.

SOME POLICE officers said Davis had split from Young Boys and was killed "over who could sell drugs in that part of town." Other officials, including Sgt. Gerald Stewart, chief of homicide unit, Squad 6, said "that definitely was not the reason."

The success of Young Boys has spawned competition from rival gangs.

Davis, Raymond Peoples and Mark Marshall are credited by police with forming Young Boys, Inc.

Peoples was shot Aug. 9 by a woman on East Philadelphia and John R. and has since been released from the hospital.

Marshall, arrested in 1974 for the murder of his father and three other persons but later acquitted, is reported to be living in Las Vegas.

'You can't leave the streets alive'

Continued from Page 1B

what's out there is real bad. We're waiting for the good stuff to come in next month. Man, we got a reputation. We're businessman and we're proud.

"Right now, the cops are hittin' us for loitering. Ain't that a trip? They can't catch us for dope. All they tryin' to do is keep us off the streets."

* * *

"WE STARTED in the Jeffries about 1976. In 1981, things in the Jeffries was real hot. It wasn't unusual to sell $7,000 to $8,000 of dope a day. We was gettin' people in from the suburbs, Canada and even Ohio. Man, we was rollin', rollin' real good.

"The cops now are trying to put the squeeze on us. But, man, it's a joke. As soon as they bust some of us and they leave, we smart up again. The people who *need* come, 'cause, man, our stuff is good.

"The police think they real smart by dressing up in baseball caps, beards and wearing army fatigues. Man, that's a joke! We all know what they look like.

"There was a time last year, one was playin' he was telephone repairman. We kept hittin' him with snowballs and tellin' him to get out.

"NOW THAT it's gettin' cold and the snow falls, we got the police beat. They can't run in that stuff and we got 'em beat. When we start runnin' they can't ke...

If it had been up to me I woulda' talked to W. and told him ta' cool out. It didn't have to be that way. We was always cool. I mean he was one of the leaders of our gang at one time. But territory is territory and you gotta' stay true to the game. He had no reason to up and just start disrespectin' us like that.

You know, I think W's biggest downfall was probably his wife Dorothy. She didn't like me, and I didn't like her. It basically stemmed outta' this time we were on the Lodge Freeway driving in Wonderful Wayne's bad ass triple black Mercedes Benz. It was the biggest Benz they had out at that time. Anyway this scraggly bitch was talkin' to him so bad that I just told him to let me out 'cause I just couldn't stand seein' nobody talk to their man like some bitch. The tramp was lettin' me know who called the shots but as it turned out her leadership was probably the cause for W.W.'s early death more than anything. I felt like me and W. was alright. I hated that W. got his cap pealed like that. But sometimes you gotta' watch who you listen to.

When Billy found out that W. had got killed he came to me and was like, "Damn dog, who took the assignment?" I said, "Man, I don't know who took that assignment. I wouldn't have given the okay on that." Billy was lookin' at it like, why I didn't give the assignment to him. But I hadn't given the assignment or the order ta' nobody. I told him I didn't know who killed him or why they killed him. All I knew was that he was in the wrong spot, from what I heard.

Billy didn't give a fuck. This guy was so loyal, it was a goddamned shame. I remember this fat guy named Huggy tried to put his blow down by runnin' specials and just tryna' run interference just about everytime I got a spot. So, I told Billy, "Everytime this fat guy finds out I got a spot, he's right there. What's up with him?" Billy says, "Man, don't worry 'bout it. I'll handle it." The next thang I knew, Billy caught up with Huggy and had a long discussion with him. After that, we never saw Huggy around no more.

Chapter 8

The Indictment

By October of 1982, I had saved five million dollars. At that point, I began to seriously think about goin' into retirement. The government didn't seem to be lettin' up and my attorney was tellin' me daily, that it was only a matter a time before they would indict me for runnin' a continual criminal enterprise. So instead of maintainin' the same attitude I'd had all along, I began to think a little more rational about my next move.

After discussing what I should do with my wife, she and I flew out to Arizona 'cause that's where we'd decided we would settle down. I didn't know anything about Phoenix, Arizona at the time. All I knew was that the sun was shinin' and it was warm out there. I didn't know that they didn't celebrate Martin Luther King's birthday or anything like that. All we wanted ta' do was go somewhere and retire.

So we set up a meetin' with Century Twenty One and met up with this real estate agent named Mr. Kilpatrick. After describin' to him the kind of house we was lookin' for, he showed us several.

After about the fourth one, we found what we were lookin' for. It was a house which sat on about three acres of the prettiest landscape that you could ever imagin'. It had a few orange trees, and a pecan tree. You just had to be there to see what I'm talkin' about.

The house was so big that it had a north wing and a south wing. It was shaped like a "Y". The master bedroom was so big, that it sat on one side all by itself. The house had cathedral ceilings, it had a den with library shelves built into the walls, a family room, where we would eventually set up our big screen television set, stereo system, and games, a dining room which looked out into nothin' but green pastures, a living room which set the whole house in motion, a big beautiful kitchen, and three bedrooms on the other side of the Y.

We got the house for one hundred and fifty thousand dollars. I knew if I had gotten a house like that in Detroit I woulda' paid at least three hundred thousand. And in California the same house would have cost about $600,000.

After we moved in, I got a one hundred channel satellite put in and a 55 inch wide screen t.v. for the family room. Plus of course, I furnished the entire house and then bought a pick up truck. The truck was just for me ta' have around the house, you know. After all this house was meant for retirement so I really didn't need all those fancy cars that would only bring attention to my house.

Before I even went to Arizona and bought the house, I had gotten telephone numbers from all the phone booths throughout Detroit, because unlike today you could call a phone booth and someone could answer it.

I would beep Slim and then put the phone booth number in and then he would go to that particular phone booth and I would call him back.

When I went on the run, that's how I stayed in touch with him.

As the months went by, the government really started increasin' their pressure on my organization. All while they were doin' this, me and Portia were flyin' back and forth from Detroit to Arizona with ten thousand dollar stacks. She'd have some stacks and I would have some. We would get on an airplane, fly out to Arizona, bury the money in the backyard of our mansion, cool out a few days, and then head back to Detroit. This went on 'til the last part of November.

By November the feds were just sittin' out in front of my house like it was their office. No longer were they tryna' just sneak around and catch me, they were just flat out waitin' in front of my house until they could get their indictment through.

Meanwhile, my attorneys were tellin' me that the government was going to indict me any day and whatever I was gonna' do, I should do it. It came back to me that on December 7th, or Pearl Harbor day, that my time was up. So, I started makin' plans ta' get the hell on outta' Detroit.

I immediately got in touch with Sylvester, who was my partner at the time, and told him that they were going to indict us on December 7th and that it was time for us to make our move. That our days as drug kingpins in Detroit were over.

S's response to me was, "Big Boy, we got too much money for these people to indict us."

I couldn't believe he'd gone that far out. I mean, we had a copula' million dollars, but we weren't Gods. I had enough sense ta' know that our time was up. It was up! Fuck all the shit I'd said in the past. Now that they'd had us for this 848 bullshit which carried life, I wasn't about ta' stick around and talk no more shit. I was out.

I told S that no matter how much money he thought he had, he could never have as much as the government. Them mothafuckas printed the money. We weren't never gone have enough money to keep us outta' jail. What you gotta' do is run bro', get out while you can, cause I'm 'bout ta' blow this mothafuckin' camp.

Instead S tried ta' talk me into stayin' in Detroit. So I called Culpepper one more time to let him know I was outty, and then I scooped up my son, my daughter, and my wife and got on outta' here. I left in November of 1982 and headed to my retirement home.

Just as my report stated, on Pearl Harbor Day the indictments came down.

S Man's name was at the top, and my name was second.

They rounded everybody up in Detroit that was considered a Young Boy. But unlike everybody else, I was sittin' back in the sun. I'd already set everybody up by tellin' them I'd bought a house in Florida and that I'd intended to retire there, so nobody really knew where I was. Even Slim my closest friend at the time was under the impression I was livin' in Florida. He didn't find out any different until he seen the area code of the number from a phone booth that I gave him and he noticed that it wasn't a Florida area code. When he saw that area code he was like, "Man, this ain't no Florida area code, what's up?"And I said, "Slim just keep it to yourself bro'. You're the only one I can let call me. You know the score bro'."

After they arrested each Young Boy, they gave them personal bonds and let 'em back on the street. Of course I wasn't even thinkin' I would be so lucky. I knew when they caught me they wasn't gone give me no personal bond.

After everybody had gone through their arraignments, I called Slim and asked Slim what I'd been charged with, 'cause he had a copy of the indictment. He told me, "Bro' it's best that you stay where you are 'cause you bein' charged with runnin' a continual crimi-

Busted

Cops seize 18 in Young Boys Inc. drug ring

By Jim Tittsworth and Don Ball
News Staff Writers

Federal agents and Detroit police continued to round up suspected managers and supervisors of the notorious Young Boys Inc. narcotics ring after a combined strike that pleased everyone from the mayor down.

Officers — armed with a federal grand jury indictment naming 41 persons, including nine women — began making arrests at dawn yesterday. They had picked up 18 suspects by last night.

THE MAIN ARREST was that of Sylvester "Seal" Murray, 30, who gave his address as Southfield. Murray allegedly is the ring's main supplier of heroin and cocaine. He was held under $10 million cash bond — the largest ever set in Federal Court in Detroit.

Another key figure named in the indictment but not yet arrested is Milton "Butch" Jones, 28, of Royal Oak Township. He is said to be the chief executive of the Young Boys distribution system, which featured street supervisors wearing beepers and $500-a-week teen-age deliverymen riding taxicabs and sometimes bicycles.

Murray and Jones, allegedly masterminds of the operation, are charged with conducting a continuing criminal enterprise. The charge could bring them 10 years to life without parole, large fines and confiscation of property. In addition, Murray is charged with evading federal income taxes on the big money he allegedly earned.

MAYOR Coleman A. Young said after the arrests, "I'm glad. If they got the top guys

Continued on Page 10A

SYLVESTER SEAL MURRAY

$10 million bail for top suspect

By Don Ball
News Staff Writer

On his way to Federal Court, Sylvester "Seal" Murray boasted to a fellow prisoner, "They're going to put a higher bond on me than DeLorean's."

The alleged main supplier of the Young Boys Inc. heroin gang came close. Federal Magistrate Paul J. Komives rejected the U.S. attorney's plea for a $15 million bond and set Murray's bond at $10 million in cash or sureties — exactly the same as that placed on John Z. DeLorean, the auto magnate facing cocaine trafficking charges in California.

Still, Murray made a mark. His bond is the highest ever

Continued on Page 10A

-A—THE DETROIT NEWS—Wednesday, Dec. 8, 1982

Cops seize 18 n drug bust

ntinued from Page 1A

Young Boys it certainly would have a vastating effect and, hopefully, a positive for us."

Federal and city law enforcement officials id the effort against Young Boys will conne, that yesterday's indictments and arsts were only the first strike.

In an allegation surfacing for the first time, e indictment states that Young Boy's drug siness extended beyond Detroit to Flint d Pontiac.

The 39 others named in the indictment are arged with assisting Jones and Murray in ansporting drugs, arranging sales, taking ephone orders. The charge against them is afficking in narcotics. Among them is Mury's sister, Denise, 25, of Detroit.

ANOTHER INDICTED but still at large Raymond Peoples, 28, of Detroit, long garded as a top leader of Young Boys but entified by federal authorities yesterday as more than middle rank.

Although all of those named in the indictent are adults, the ring employed boys in eir early teens or even younger to make liveries. The best delivery boys received nuses which included Mercedes Benz cars, ld and diamond-studded jewelry, leather ckets and 10-speed bicycles, police said.

The use of juveniles, combined with strict scipline which investigators said included urder, and the organization's pyramidal mmand structure helped shield leaders like urray and Jones from police penetration in e past, a federal official said.

Unlike low-level adult drug pushers, who ght be turned into informers under threat long prison terms, the Young Boys' juveles were often held only briefly in the couny youth home and then released without fear further punishment, police said.

A NUMBER OF guns (as well as some rcotics, jewelry and cash) were confiscated ring yesterday's arrests. Detroit police said at the confiscated weapons will be checked see if they match bullets taken from victs of unsolved murders.

Detroit Police Chief William L. Hart said to 150 federal, state and local officers rked for more than two years on the intgation that resulted in the indictments.

Insp. Raymond Murray of the Detroit Po Department narcotics section, said, "The ople I would like to recognize in all of this the Detroit and federal undercover offis who obviously can't be here.

"Without them we wouldn't have a case."

ROBERT DeFAUW, Detroit director of U.S. Drug Enforcement Administration, imated that Young Boys had the capabil of selling up to $1 million worth of heroin d cocaine weekly. But other law enforcent officials cautioned that it was unlikely s volume of sales could be sustained week er week.

DeFauw noted that more than $1.3 million

NEWS PHOTO/ DUANE E. BELANGER

Handcuffed youths enter police headquarters after raid.

List of 41 indicted by U.S. jury

The following 41 men and women were named yesterday in federal indictments as members of the narcotics organization Young Boys Inc.:

Sylvester "Seal" Murray, Milton David "Butch" Jones, Velma Bailes, Maurice Bell, Steven Andre Brown, Karen "Kim" Brown.

Eli Carter; Betty Crawford, alias Betty Mallory, Ferrar Crawford, Emanuel Cromer, Ida Mae Chapman; Herbert Daniels, Richard Daniels; Melvin Davenport, also known as Samuel Livingston or "Sammy D."

Andre Diggs, John "Creeper" Doe, Ardie Mae Easterly, John Fullivova, Celos "Pete" Fulwylie, Keith Futtrell, Maurice Gibbs, Karl Gatlin, also known as "Pratt."

Ricky Humphries; Michael "Big Mike" Jenkins, Alonzo Long, Rodney Mason, Lewis McClaine; Denise Murray, Curtis Napier, Timothy Peoples, Raymond Peoples.

George Sanders; Art Sellars, Virdell "Bonnie" Shipp, Tamara Sparks, Paul Smith; Portia Sturdivant, alias Portia Jones, James Thorpe, John Thomas, Kevin Wilson, Darryl Young.

federal official said.

Although Young Boys Inc. is believed by police to have formed as early as 1978 in the 10th (Livernois) Precinct, the federal indictment alleges that it became a widespread conspiracy with branches in Highland Park, Pontiac and Flint in 1980.

U.S. Attorney Leonard Gilman said the arrests which started yesterday mark "the culmination of the first phase of a continuing investigation into the narcotics traffic in Detroit and southeastern Michigan."

News staff writer Earl Dowdy contributed to this report.

Lawmen's 'odd couple' led drug ring roundup

By Jim Tittsworth and Dinah Eng
News Staff Writers

One barks. One purrs. Together, they put the bite on Young Boys Inc.

Robert DeFauw, chief of the U.S. Drug Enforcement Agency office in Detroit, and Insp. Raymond Murray, head of the Detroit Police Department's narcotics section, put together the operation that snagged the alleged major supplier and chief executive of the drug ring yesterday.

On the surface, the two men are opposites.

DeFauw, 48, is a stocky, barrel-chested man with the voice of a bullhorn. Murray, 43, is a tall, muscular fellow with a soft, patient, serious manner.

Flash and daring are DeFauw's style. Murray is methodical, a conservative dresser who looks more like an insurance salesman than a cop.

BOTH ARE NATIVE Detroiters and career cops.

DeFauw grew up in an east side family of Belgian extraction. He saw some action overseas as a marine during the Korean War.

He returned home to join the Detroit Police Department in 1955 and spent five years on the street. In the early '60s, he joined the Drug Enforcement Agency and traveled the world — to Europe, Africa and the Mediterranean. He was involved in international efforts to destroy heroin processing plants in Marseilles, France.

He was appointed regional DEA director for Southeast Asia, and one of his favorite activities was sweeping the Thailand jungle in a fast-moving helicopter busting hidden heroin laboratories.

A picture of one of those raids hangs in his Detroit office. It shows DeFauw with a big grin on his face while the heroin lab burns in the background.

"I LIKE TAKING these people down," says DeFauw of narcotics traffickers. "It's a challenge.

"They're slick and they're the scum of the earth. They destroy the wills and minds of the youth of this country, and I can think of no better calling.

"I enjoy taking them down."

Murray, a Wayne State University graduate, was a lieutenant for three years in the Wayne County Organized Crime Task Force before budget cutbacks eliminated his job. He then spent six months working for the Detroit Police Department's organized crime and homicide sections before being promoted to head of the narcotics section.

MURRAY LIKES to work with the big picture rather than the pieces. When he became inspector in narcotics last year, Murray said:

"The only way to get Young Boys Inc. is by conducting a long-range investigation aimed at the top, where you can document the buys and the conspiracy to traffic, where you can dot every *i* and cross every *t*."

Vessel passages

DETROIT
Upbound yesterday

A.M. — Henry Ford II (ar), 1:15; Calcite II, 1:50; Red Wing, 4:10; Frankcliffe Hall, 7:10; Canadian Progress, 7:55; Scott Misener, 10:20.

P.M. — Georgian Bay, 12:20; Golden Hind, 2:50; Doan Transport, 3:40; Black Bay, 4:05; Simcoe, 6:00; Saturn (ar), 7:30; Eastern Shell, 7:40; Lake Manitoba, 7:45; Canadian Mariner, 7:55; Jupiter, 9:50; Algowood, 10:45; Henry Ford II (ar), 11:15.

Downbound yesterday

A.M. — Hassell, 1:15; Anangel Fortuna, 2:00; Pineglen (ar), 4:45; Tug John Purvis & Barge, 8:15; Sophia M., 8:45; Henry Ford II (cl), 9:10; Sava, 10:30.

P.M. — Eglantine, 12:45; Canadian Hunter, 1:40; Cobetas, 1:35; Tug Malcolm & STR C.L. Austin & Tug Barbra Ann, 3:05; Cartiercliffe Hall, 4:00; Soodoc, 4:15; Baie St Paul, 5:10; Tug Olive L. Moore Barge Buckeye (cl), 5:15; Ruder Boskovic (ar), 5:20; American Republic (ar), 6:35; Antonio Maceo, 6:50; Tarantau, 8:25; Ruder Boskovic (cl), 9:00; Canadian Pioneer, 9:45; John O. McKellar, 10:20; American Republic (cl), 10:30.

(ar) — arrived; (cl) — cleared

nal enterprise and they plan on given you life."

Two or three days after that, Slim told me the news had reported me as being in Florida and that they had put together a task force to head down there ta' get me.

The feds rounded up between seventy ta' eighty D.E.A., FBI, and U.S. Marshals to flood Florida with my picture with the intent of draggin' me back ta' Detroit. But little did they know, I was at home in Arizona eatin' oranges from my tree and kickin' it in the sun with my family. I had no intentions of ever poppin' up again.

After they couldn't find me in Florida, they came out with a ten thousand dollar reward, and put it on tv and in the newspapers. The way they had it set up was that the person could tell on me and didn't have to worry about nothin' cause they could keep their identity secret. People were callin' in with all kinds of tips tryna' turn me in. But I just sat back 'cause like I said, I didn't give a fuck. The only person who knew where I was, was Slim.

While all of this was going on, I was callin' my attorneys Wilford Rice and Culpepper everyday askin' them what was up and what an 848 consisted of. I was tryna' get a feel for the kinda' time I was lookin' at.

Each day that I talked to Slim, I told him that there was nothin' keepin' us from rollin' but us and that if he wanted to keep rollin' it was up to him. But I wasn't comin' back to Detroit.

At that point I felt like the deck was stacked up

Drug source next target, agents say

By Jim Tittsworth
and Don Ball
News Staff Writers

Major blows struck at Detroit's Young Boys Inc. drug ring will be followed by renewed efforts to neutralize the city's suppliers of heroin and cocaine, federal officials say.

One of the ring's alleged founders, Sylvester "Seal" Murray is in custody with nearly a score of suspected underlings. And law enforcement agencies across the country are seeking Murray's reputed chief lieutenant, Milton "Butch" Jones.

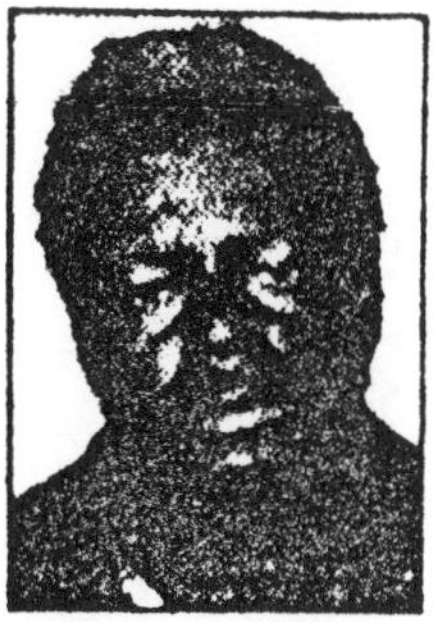

Milton Jones

THEY WERE AMONG 41 persons accused this week by a federal grand jury in Detroit of sharing in a narcotics operation.

$10,000 reward set for Young Boys boss

By Don Ball
News Staff Writer

The government is offering a $10,000 reward for information leading to the arrest of Milton David "Butch" Jones, accused of being the head of Detroit's Young Boys Inc. dope ring.

Jones, 28, of Oak Park, is charged with running the ring which employed an estimated 300 persons in a multimillion-dollar heroin-and-cocaine operation in the metropolitan area.

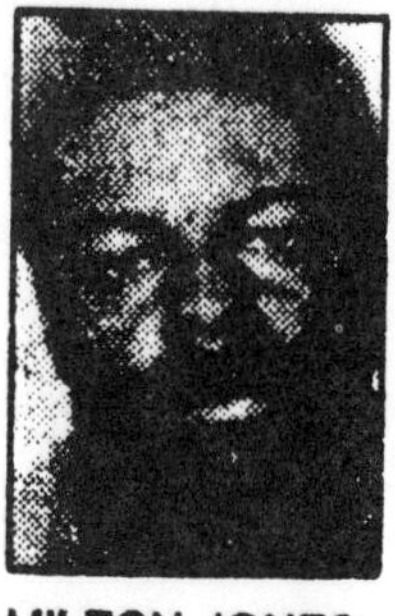
MILTON JONES

He has been sought since Dec. 7 when agents of the U.S. Drug Enforcement Administration (DEA) and Detroit police began rounding up 39 persons indicted on drug conspiracy charges.

SYLVESTER "Seal" Murray, the 30-year-old wholesale supplier for Young Boys, was among the 31 persons arrested. Murray is held on a $10-million cash bond.

Seven others charged in the case also are fugitives, including Jones' girl friend, Portia Jones Sturdivant.

Robert J. DeFauw, special agent in charge of the Detroit DEA office, said $2,000 rewards each have been posted for information leading to the arrest of Ms. Sturdivant and the other six fugitives.

They are Darryl Young, 25, reportedly Murray's right-hand man; Karen Brown, 24; Richard Daniels, 19; Andre Diggs, 21; Ardie Mae Easterly, no age given; and Tamara Sparks, 30. All are from Detroit.

"Anyone with information about the fugitives should contact either my office at 226-7290, or the narcotics unit of the Detroit police at 224-4323," DeFauw said. "The identity of persons giving information will be kept secret."

IN THE INDICTMENT, Jones was charged with obtaining heroin and supervising on a daily basis the packaging and distribution of the narcotic to a network of street salesmen, usually juveniles who could not be charged in adult court because of their age.

One informant told an undercover DEA agent that Young Boys averaged $50,000 daily in sales.

against me, so I had no intent of playing out my whole hand. At that time, I was content with being with my family and enjoyin' the millions I had saved.

After about ninety days went by, I called Betty and told her to go and see two lawyers. Richard Zimser and Richard Lustick. They were some attorneys outta' Southfield that came highly recommended for federal cases.

At the particular time, this Jewish guy named Leonard Gillman was the U.S. Attorney. Zimser, and Lustick were both Jewish.

I always knew that the only obligation a Jew has, is to another Jew. I firmly believed that and still do. As it turned out, Richard Lustick, the attorney I hired, knew U.S. Attorney Leonard Gillman so because of that I began my negotiations through Richard Lustick.

After I sent Lustick down there ta' talk to the U.S. Attorney, he told me that if I turned myself in I could get a fifteen year plea, I said I wasn't doin' no fifteen years, let 'em keep lookin' for me.

I said, "You gone have to go back down there and negotiate a better plea than that."

So, I called him back again the next day, and he told me that they would consider givin' me a thirteen year no parole plea if I turned myself in the next day. So, I asked him what kinda' pleas was they givin' everybody else.

I asked him how much time would Betty, Portia, Tamara, Ollie May, Slim, Kethon, Moe Heart, Dead Eye, Richie Rich, Kirk, my cousin, and a few other guys would get if I turned myself in. I was tryna" find out if I turned myself in, would the government be lenient on the rest of my codefendants.

The U.S. Attorney then told my attorney that he was not gone be manipulated by me. That they would catch me eventually.

So I told my attorney, Richard Lustick, "Thirteen years was an unlucky number and I wasn't goin' ta' jail with no thirteen year sentence. Tell the U.S. Attorney, no deal. I ain't turnin' myself in."

After two or three days I called him back and he said that he had gotten it down to twelve years, with no cooperation, no parolable sentence. If I turned myself in immediately and started doin' my time.

He said, "That's it."

So I asked Lustick to put it in writin' and I would be on my way. The catch was that the assigned judge had to accept my twelve year plea but if he didn't he would have to allow me to post a fifty thousand dollar cash bond.

The way the plea was set up was by Rule 11. I had everything documented includin' my plea. After they had put my plea in writin', I asked Culpepper to look it over. After he read it over he then read it to me over the phone.

I've got the plea in my hands now so I'll read it to you in the same way that he read it ta' me back then. It goes: "Criminal number 82-80591, Violation Title 21 USC, Offense. Engaging In A Continual Criminal Enterprise, Statutory Maximum Penalty -Life Imprisonment, One Hundred Thousand Dollar Fine and Forfeiture of Profits, Interests, and any Property obtained in such enterprise. Rule 11 plea agreement on count 38- the maximum term shall not exceed the twelve years, C. the following offender's charge shall be dismissed pursuit to 11E1A, count 1 of indictment at sentencing dismissed." That was the conspiracy charged.

Then it states: "D. the following additional promises has been made for the attorney by the government. All parties recognize the defendants refusal to cooperate with the government. However, the government reserves the right to call the defendant before grand jury. If said action is taken it will be taken in connection with only one grand jury." That was my pleas agreement. Robert M. Morgan was the prosecutor in the case.

After much contemplation on my own, me and my wife discussed what would be best for me. To either turn myself in or to stay on the run.

Now, keep in mind I had an eight year old son, and a three year old daughter. I knew that if I tried to put 'em in school in Phoenix their records from Detroit Public Schools would be transferred and the federal government would eventually track me down, through my kids, to Arizona. So, Portia agreed that I should go and take the plea.

Richard Lustick's fee for arrangin' the plea was fifty thousand dollars. The day before I turned myself in, I took him his fifty thousand in cash. I also took him twenty-five thousand for Portia's case, twenty-five thousand for Betty's case, and twenty-five thousand for Tamara's case. So, he let Richard Zimser, another brilliant attorney, handle Portia's, Betty's, and Tamara's case.

On March 22, 1983, me and Betty went down to the Federal Building and turned ourselves in. Attorney Lustick was with us. After we got there, they took us downstairs to the marshals, fingerprinted us, and gave us our numbers. My federal number was 04122-039. My state number was 140833 Jones. That's how they usually refer to a person. They usually call you by the last three numbers. In the federal system, I was 04122-039 Jones. In the state system I was referred to as 833 Jones. After they fingerprinted me, they took me upstairs to arraign me on the indictment and I entered my plea in front of Judge Ralph B. Guy, Jr.

When I'd entered my plea, and the judge asked me why I was pleading guilty and what I had done, I told Judge Guy that I was the organizer, supervisor, and the manager of Young Boys Incorporated. I told him when I'd bought those cars from S., that he had no knowledge that it was with drug money. That was the way I wanted it.

I wanted it on record that he didn't have nothin' to do with my organization. I wanted to take the weight for the narcotic rein. That was the way I played it, 'cause like I said, I'm a soldier. The buck stops here.

S was a religious God-fearin' and nonviolent man. He had nothin' ta' do with all the violence and killings

Drug Boss Surrenders

By TIM BELKNAP
Free Press Staff Writer

Milton (Butch) Jones, one of the two alleged top leaders of the Young Boys Inc. heroin ring, surrendered to federal authorities in Detroit Tuesday and pleaded guilty in U.S. District Court to conducting a criminal enterprise.

"You're Milton David Jones?" asked U.S. District Judge Ralph Guy Jr.

"Yes, sir," replied the stocky, 27-year-old man dressed in a blue and gray jogging suit and white track shoes.

That brief conversation ended the running days of Jones, who had been one of the most hunted fugitives in Michigan for more than three months.

Jones, 27, of Oak Park, was placed in an unspecified prison in lieu of a $10 million cash bond to await sentencing at a date yet to be set.

IF A plea-bargaining agreement is approved by Guy, Jones will serve no more than 12 years in prison. The charge carries a minimum sentence of 10 years in prison with no parole sentence and a maximum sentence of life imprisonment and a $100,000 fine.

Under the agreement, Jones is not required to co-operate with the government, and he will not have to testify against his more than 20 alleged former accomplices in a trial scheduled to start April 25 before Guy.

Jones

A charge of conspiring to possess heroin with the intent to distribute was dropped. It carried a 15-year prison term and a $25,000 fine.

JONES HAD BEEN a fugitive with a $10,000 reward on his head since Dec. 6, 1982, when he and 40 other alleged upper- and middle-level leaders of Young Boys Inc. were indicted by a federal grand jury.

His surrender came after complex negotiations in the past two weeks between defense attorneys Richard Zipser and Rick Lustig and U.S. Attorney Leonard Gilman and Assistant U.S. Attorney Robert Morgan, according to court documents.

For security reasons, the surrender was kept secret until Jones walked into Guy's well-guarded courtroom in downtown Detroit, accompanied by Lustig and Betty Crawford, 39, of Detroit, a companion of Jones.

Crawford pleaded guilty to a conspiracy count in a plea-bargaining deal in which she admitted to having been a cocaine dealer for Young Boys.

Despite the fact that police using sophisticated spying equipment were supposed to have key suspects under surveillance 24 hours before their arrests, Jones escaped the massive raids Dec. 6 and 7 that resulted in the arrests of most of Young Boys' alleged leaders.

HIS ALLEGED partner, Sylvester "Seal" Murray, 30, of Southfield, was arrested and charged with conducting a continuing criminal enterprise and conspiracy.

Informants told police that Jones made all the decisions for Young Boys operations and that Murray was in charge of obtaining heroin, according to court documents. Jones told Guy Tuesday that he was the "organizer, supervisor, and manager" of the drug operation.

The ring, which police estimate had about 350 members, many of them juveniles, grossed about $7.5 million a week in heroin sales, prosecutors said.

that went on. I was runnin' the organization before he ever came about. So I virtually took the weight for everythang. And to tell you the truth, I was tryna' take some weight off my man S, 'cause he had never been ta' jail.

After I'd turned myself in, the government made deals with the rest of my crew and gave most of them twenty-seven month pleas.

Na', I'ma' tell you, I don't know how this shit happened, but my boy Raymond Peoples, who the government, and everybody else had accused of being one of the original creators of Young Boy's only ended up gettin' an eighteen month sentence. I don't wanna' believe that he broke bad but what else could explain it. What else could explain how the very person who many newspaper articles had mentioned, numerous times, in the same breath as me could get only a few months.

But fuck it, he was my boy Timmie's brother, and Timmie was alright with me so I'll just leave it at that.

After that, they took me to Milan and immediately put me in D block, which was segregated for all marshal prisoners. I was considered a marshal prisoner, 'cause I hadn't been sentenced yet. When I got there, S. Man, Dead Eye, Butch Rod, and Cromer was already there. I think they were the only ones down there. The rest of my codefendants were over in E block, I think.

About two or three weeks later, they caught Richie Rich. He'd let his so called boy, Lughead get him a motel room and as soon as he stepped into the room, the

Young Boys 'enforcer' believed slaying victim

Raymond W. Peoples, an alleged leader of the notorious Young Boys Inc. drug ring, was tentatively identified by police as the victim of a fatal shooting last night in Detroit.

Details of the shooting incident were sketchy and a positive identification of the victim had not been made. However, homicide detectives said they "had reason to believe" the victim is Peoples.

Peoples, 28, was described by police more than two years ago as a top "enforcer" for the Young Boys ring. The ring, which relied on juveniles as its drug runners, sold an estimated $50,000 worth of heroin and cocaine daily until it was broken up in a massive police raid in December 1982.

Five months later, Peoples was sentenced to prison after pleading guilty in Federal Court in Detroit to a charge of conspiring to sell heroin and cocaine.

In August 1982, Peoples was shot in the chest and back while talking to two men on a Detroit street.

Peoples had an extensive police record dating from 1975, when he and two other men were charged with beating to death a man with broken concrete in a racial altercation. He was acquitted on that charge after three trials.

— *By Mike Wowk*

police popped up and arrested him. Till this day, I don't think Richie Rich ever knew that Lughead was the one who turned him in.

Not everybody from the Young's Boy's got indicted. My man Stoney Roney, who I use ta' give large quantities of cocaine to, after S Man would give it to me, never got indicted. Stoney was one of the guys who held down the east side for us. It was cool that he didn't get indicted though because I knew when I went ta' jail that I could still get money through him.

My Family

Portia Jones *(My Wife)*:

When I first met my husband I was fifteen. He was livin' on Monterey and I was livin' in Highland Park on Louise Street. I thought Butch was a gambler, because everytime I would see him, he and his friends would be shootin' dice under the streetlights. It would be Black Joe, Al Baby, Sid the Kid, and Black Bart.

I didn't know that he sold dope, because he was always gamblin' when I was around him, but I did know that he kept a gun at all times.

We had a lot of fun together. He would take me to the show, then we would go out ta' eat. We would catch cabs everywhere we went, because we didn't have a car at the time.

One day he came to me and asked me to type a note for him. When he told me what he wanted me to type, I asked him why and it seemed like his whole expression changed. It was like talkin' with somebody I didn't know. He told me again, "Type the note like I goddamned said."

So, I went on and typed:"This is a stick-up. Don't make it a murder. Put all the money in the bag and won't nobody get hurt." I typed the note and gave it to him. Then Sid the Kid and Nate the Great came to pick him up.

About two hours later all three of them came back with bags of money. They poured it on the bed in my bedroom and started countin' the money and splittin' it up. I don't know how much they got outta' the robbery, but he gave me $10,000 to put up, plus he had some money left in his pocket.

I had never seen that much money in my life before that night.

When he came back home that night I asked him what did they rob. He told me to shutup and don't worry about it.

Come to find out, him, Nate, and Sid were robbin' banks. I ended up typing up about eight or nine more notes and they always came to split the money up in Highland Park.

After awhile, I had saved up about fifty thousand dollars. I had it in five shoe boxes tucked away in my closet under some dirty clothes. Butch had bought a brand new Mark IV. Plus he had bought a lot of clothes for him and me and we began making plans to buy a house, 'cause I was pregnant with Mo-Mo at that time.

Then, he got into trouble. He and Leroy killed somebody on Hamilton in Highland Park. About six months after that, the police caught him. He went ta' jail and ended up gettin' seven and a half ta' fifteen for manslaughter.

My son was born two weeks after Butch got locked up. Out of everything about our life, this is what I remember most, because I was so young and so disappointed that our life had ended up that way.

Mo Mo Jones *(My Son)*:

When we were stayin' on Barrett, I can remember times when my daddy would come home at night with garbage bags full of money. I was just a youngster and he would want me to count it. I would count it 'til I passed out. I also remember holdin' the envelopes, while he put the mixed jive in the envelopes. All my life I've been more advanced than anyone my age. When I was young, they called me Top Dog, 'cause I was a dog and I'm gonna' always be a dog.

I wanted to be a big fellow, like the rest of the crew. I remember this time, when the police raided the house on Barrett. The police were tryna' interrogate me about my daddy, but my daddy had already taught me when I was growin' up not to tell the police shit. And I did just that. All I had to say was, "My name is Jamakay Jones and my attorney is Otis Culpepper."

I remember another time that my father had this house on Chelsey where most of the Y.B.I., that was somebody, stayed.

One day the police raided there and tried the same shit. All I had to say was, "My name is Jamakay Jones. My attorney is Otis Culpepper."

They tried pushin' and hittin' me, 'cause I was young. It wasn't nothin' happenin'. They were tellin' me that I was goin' to juvenile 'til I was sixteen or twenty-one and all that shit, but wasn't nothin' happenin'.

I also remember how one day me and my dad were ridin' home in a burgundy Vette and this old big car was followin' us. It must've been an L.T.D. I still remember it, like it was yesterday. They was followin' us and he had peeped it out. So, he called home and told my mother, "Portia get the heaters out. I'm on my way." He called her from the car phone and told her to have the heaters by the door. He dropped me off, got the heaters and got back in the car. He left with the heaters.

A bunch of years later, I just happened to ask him about that and he said that it was taken care of.

When everybody went to Cedar Point, I was there. It was like Vette city. Everybody was in a Vette. Everybody went to Cedar Point with those campaign hats and Adidas on with a bunch of money. I was just a little young nigga'. It was on. We went to Cedar Point and had a ball. Everybody was tight then.

As I was growin' up, I started peepin' out that a lot of guys weren't for the right thang. I peeped the shadiness outta' 'em when I was young. Everybody that I thought wasn't right turned out not to be right. Lughead wasn't right. I knew he wasn't right. I never liked him anyway. Richie Rich wasn't right. Look how it is now. I was peepin' that out when I was young and I turned out ta' be right. A whole bunch of different individuals wasn't right. A lot of them guys felt like they wanted to be "The Guy".

I remember when daddy gave a party on that yacht. He was dressed up like a sailor man. Everybody was havin' fun. It was a little fuckin' goin' on on the boat. They didn't think that I knew that by me bein' so young. I don't even know if he knew. Everybody had fun.

All while I was growin' up, my daddy would always show me the ropes, the real way, uncut. He taught me street knowledge. But he also taught me to be school smart too. He always kept it real.

Some of the stuff he put me up on was stuff like drivin'. He used to let me drive his Benzes, Lincolns and all that before I was ten years old.

We use to fight dogs in Ardie Mae's house next door. She used to live next door to my Granny. I used to fight pits in the basement. Once we even had a kennel built. It was sixteen Pits in all and one or two Rottweilers. All of em were killers, too. They were straight-up killers.

We use to swim. We did that in the house in Oak Park with a swimming pool with a dome over it and we would swim no matter what the weather was. When I was young, that was the shit. I liked that, ya' know.

Man, I remember this time, when we had a pool party. Me, Baby Ray, Apple Jack, and whole bunch of others went to the store. We were about two cars deep. I was ridin' with Ray and 'em. We went to a store out in Oak Park in Benzes. They ended up wantin' ta' ride out to Palmer Park so we rode out to Palmer Park and picked up two girls who we had just met. They were all in. Then, we went to an apartment. It must've been Raymond's apartment. It was about six guys, includin' me. Them girls were freaky live. We got freaky with 'em. I was just a young guy gettin' freaky with them girls. You couldn't tell me nothin'. They were all on a guy, ya' know. It was a straight-up fuck fest. Shit, that was before I could even bust a nut, ya' know.

I remember that we had got this house in Phoenix, Arizona. This was durin' the time that he was wanted. It was a mansion. It had a satellite with thirty or forty thousand dollars worth of furniture. When we was there, we told my lil' sister that we were in Florida, 'cause she was real young and would be talkin' on the phone with my grandmother or auntie for instance and she might've said, "I'm in Phoenix."

So, we told her that we were in Florida. That's where she thought we was. When we stayed there, I remember helpin' him bury some money in the back of our house outside.

I guess it was months later that we came back to Michigan. I think he was still in Arizona. I remember one day my grandmother said, "Yeah, Butch was here last night. He went ta' turn himself in."

At the time, it was snow on the ground and I just went outside and laid in the snow. I was like, "Damn, my daddy is gone ta' jail." I just laid in the snow, face first. It was like my whole world was crushed, 'cause after he got locked up nothin' was ever again the same.

But I have to add, when he was out, man it was on.

Chapter 9

Rickey Peoples

Interview with Rickey Peoples

Interviewer	How old were you when you joined Y.B.I?
Rickey	In my twenties.
Interviewer	When did you meet Butch? How long have you known him?
Rickey	I've been knowin' him every since the early seventies.
Interviewer	How old were you when you met him?
Rickey	I had to be goin' on twenty-five. We used to gamble together.

Interviewer	Is your mother and father in prison for participatin' in the young boy's organization?
Rickey	Yeah, my mother is doing twenty to forty and my father, who was doin' about the same amount of time died before he could finish doin' his time.
Interviewer	Jesus!
Rickey	And my sister is in there too.
Interviewer	So your whole family was in the organization, huh.?
Rickey	Yeah, you know gettin' back to Butch, the thang that I liked most about him was that he had great insight for bein' able to pick a guy's category. You know, where you fit in. A lot of people underestimated him. He was the kinda' guy that only said somethin' once. And if he said it, he meant that it should be done just that way. If you did what you were told, then you got rewarded for it. And if you didn't...
Interviewer	You guys believed in honor and respect?
Rickey	Yeah. Most definitely. You had to have honor and respect.
Interviewer	So, you all were like the Black Mafia.

Rickey	So to speak, we had principles and values amongst each other. I had to want to see you do better in order for me to do better. We honored that.
	But then the third generation came. That's where the guns came in at. The organization had grew so much that a lot of people were in it that we didn't even know. They were doin' things that we didn't find out about 'til maybe two or three weeks after the shit was done.
Interviewer	So would you say that the organization grew outta' control?
Rickey	Yeah. It kinda' got out of hand.
	The guys in the Brewster Projects was jealous of us and at night they'd get up on the roofs and shoot at us. Blaw! Blaw! Blaw!
	My job in the organization was to distribute the drugs. Every mornin' at 6:30 a.m. I'd be sittin' at my window lookin' out and all at once, about fifteen cabs would pull up.
	Those were the lieutenants. They would all come around in the mornin' in cabs to pick up their bags. The bags would be five, ten, twenty, and thirty thousand dollar bags.

At 7:30 p.m., when they would return, they would come to turn in the money. All that they didn't sell, they took to the motherland, which was Dexter. I gotta' admit that it was a real organized operation. Big Boy had it all under control.

Like I said, Butch knew how ta' pick people for whatever postitions they were fit for. That's where this guy named Timmy Peoples came in at. He was goin' ta' school and came in one day from college. Butch seen that he could count good and Butch jumped on it.

Timmy was more like a sergeant. He put him at the top of the regime that counted the money, but eventually I think Timmie outgrew himself.

See, Butch's nephew, Lil' Moe's job was to stay with Timmy and watch what he did, but Timmy out thought him. Moe couldn't out think Timmy.

He would come to me and say, "Timmie, gave me thirty thousand. I'm goin' ta' take my crew shoppin'." But Timmy would come and get sixty thousand, 'cause he kept up with the real big things. He would figure out how to make money off of money. Like if he had what was suppose to be a hundred thousand dollars worth of shit, he'd find a way to make a hundred and fifty thousand off it.

That's how come you'd look up and he'd have a bank roll.

Anyway, back to the cabs. Everybody came in cabs, 'cause if you came in cabs you could beat the case, 'cause any mothafucka could have left the dope in the cab. See, even the cab drivers were on the payroll. We made Unity Cabs rich. Plus, we had a restaurant on the corner called Milos and everybody that came to buy narcotics had to buy hamburgers. We called them monster burgers. Milo's was so huge that it made thousands of dollars sellin' them burgers.

Butch was real firm against us hangin' out in clubs, 'cause all blind spots were hit spots. See a lot of people were jealous of us so anything we did, we did amongst the family.

But, don't get me wrong, we wanted to go out like all the other guys. We wanted to go to the titty bars and stuff like that, but that was a no-no, a violation. He didn't like that, and if one of us would go, he would take their car. A lot of guys would call Butch and say, "Man, your boy so and so is down here at the joint". Like Kirk McGurk and Richie Rich, you know, who were known killers. They didn't have no business bein' in those kinda' blind spots. So, if Butch heard you had been in one of those spots, then he'd penalize you.

One time, all the top of the regime was stealin', doin' a lot of petty stuff, and Butch found out. He had just bought 'em all Mercedes and it hurt him that they was stealin' from him. He went over there and went to whippin' everybody. He beat everyone of 'em and stripped 'em. The next thing you knew, Kethon was ridin' down the street on a bicycle. Butch was like, "These mothafuckas been stealin' from me no tellin' how long and I ain't havin' it." So he took all their cars. He took about six Mercedes. He took John John's, Moe Heart's, Kethon's. He let Kirk keep his only because he'd just joined and he felt like everybody had led him on.

Kirk was a young guy. This was during the time that Kirk was suppose to have threatened Mayor Coleman Young in a letter. But at that time, Kirk couldn't even

Mayor vows war on young pushers

By Robert E. Roach
News Staff Writer

Youthful drug dealers — such as those in the notorious Young Boys Inc. heroin ring — "must be taken off the street," according to Detroit Mayor Coleman A. Young.

He called the drug situation "most serious" yesterday in discussing Young Boys Inc. and its possible connection with the slaying last month of a Detroit police officer assigned to investigate youth gangs.

The mayor said he would consider calling for expenditure of additional public funds to counteract the widespread street sale operations.

Police believe the adults who finance Young Boys Inc. use juvenile boys as salesmen because of their immunity from prosecution as adults if arrested. The state's Juvenile Code lets juvenile drug salesmen off with minimum punishment or, often, no punishment at all, police say.

Hinting that public money might have to be spent for buildings to hold the city's new breed of youthful criminals, Young said:

"I think it would be cheaper to isolate them and attempt to rehabilitate them than to turn them loose on the street again, where they will undoubtedly cause much more social and actual dollars-and-cents damage."

Young's comments came after his annual budget address.

In that talk, he said violent crime in Detroit is down 14 percent overall and major crime has declined 22 percent since 1976, compared to a 33 percent increase nationally.

"The message of these hard statistics is clear: There is no crime wave in Detroit," he said.

write. That was another play by Baby Ray. See Baby Ray was the one who'd put that hit out on the mayor. It was a play that Baby Ray did to try to get him outta' the way.

Interviewer	Where did people get that rumor that Baby Ray was the leader of the Young Boys at first?
Rickey	Because he was one of the ones that was with him when we first started out.
Interviewer.	So, him and Butch was cool.
Rickey	Right, but Butch caught a little case when they were younger and went to jail.
Interviewer	Which one, the one in Highland Park?
Rickey	Yeah.
Interviewer	Butch shot the boy in '73 and did those four years. So, Butch knew Baby Ray before he went in. Then when he went in Baby Ray got the raw thang goin', right?
Rickey	Yea, but, it was never off the ground like it was when Butch came home. And when Butch came home, Raymond got jealous but he tried not to show it, 'cause Butch was still showin' him love. Butch was givin' Baby Ray positions. One time Baby Ray went outta' town with sixty or

seventy-thousand and Butch had to send for him, 'cause somebody had robbed him. He went outta' town to get a connect. After that, Baby Ray didn't get no respect from nobody.

The way that Butch would pay off his people would be, for example, everybody would meet up at Diddley's Bar on six mile. I mean about three hundred people would show up and Butch would have a big box of money and just start passin' it out. He'd call off, "Dexter. Then Brewster. Then Joy Road." You know. He did it like that.

He'd give maybe eight thousand to one guy to pay his crew, five thousand for another, eight thousand to another. Then he'd have cases and cases of Remy Martin. Everybody had Remy's. Plus he'd order girls.

See, this is how we partied, so that's why he felt that nobody should ever have to go to no blind spots. But even still, when some of the younger guys would leave to go home, the older guys would stick 'em up, so that was fucked up, you know.

Interviewer They were sticking the lieutenants up?

Rickey Yeah.

Interviewer Is that an example of what you meant by people stealin'.

Rickey Man, the old players would stick the young ones up and then the younger players began plottin' against the old ones. And the money had gotten so large that many days we would go well over a hundred thousand dollars and Butch would be layin' up in this ol' mansion and money would just be comin' in. I'll never forget it.

The only thing Butch would say was, "Just put it in the safe. Just put it in the safe." Sometimes the safe would be too full and we couldn't put the money in the safe.

I remember when we would be at a house countin' money and Butch would tell you to count the tens, another person would count the fives, and another person counted the twenties. Everybody would count their bundles up to a thousand and then wrap it.

I remember one time, I counted one million dollars. It took all night, 'cause it was comin' off the streets in singles. We would just take the singles and put 'em in a big ol' box. We used to buy cars, pistols, and

	pay the rent with the singles.
Interviewer	Let's go back to the cab scene. Did the money all come back like it was supposed to?
Rickey	Well, a lot of things might happen through the course of a day. A guy might get stuck-up or go to jail or whatever, but it didn't matter, he still had to be accountable for that money. Everybody was accountable for what happened in that week.
Interviewer	They either showed the money or the dope.
Rickey	Right.
Interviewer	What if he went to jail with the dope on him, then what?
Rickey	He shouldn't have had that much dope on him.
Interviewer	What if he went ta' jail with the money on him?
Rickey	The money and the dope should have never been in the same place, and the person should have never gotten busted with any less than two bundles on him. So any more than that then he had to pay.
Rickey	You gotta realize, we had people out there

makin' twenty ta' thirty thousand a month so this shit was no joke.

We would go to the Parliament and the Funkadelics concerts and everybody would pull up in limousines. All of us. We'd order maybe fifteen limo's. Man we would be so out there that everybody thought we were the ones in the concert. People would be like, "Who is that? Are those the entertainers? But because we all wore red and white some people knew who we were.

Interviewer Red and white were you guys' colors?

Rickey Yea. But you know man, even Butch got way out there, I remember goin' to Butch one day and tellin' him how things was really gettin' outta' hand. I told him, "Big Boy, things happenin' in the street that you don't know about, that we gotta' curve."

His reply was, "Rickey, I can beat anything but gettin' caught red handed murderin' somebody." Man, Butch was gone, too. He was a young black kid outta' the ghetto who'd become a millionaire off of sellin' dope. He had gotten' so big that he bought his attorney Culpepper a Rolls Royce for beatin' a case for him. A Rolls Royce, man! He was like Robin Hood. He was just givin' people money, ya' know. I used to tell my brother, "Damn man, that man is a good guy". He looked out. All his captains stayed in lavish houses. We even had a gold and bronze pool table with Y.B.I engraved on it. It was laid. It was right over on Chelsey on the east side. Then, we had houses so that if the kids were livin' on the street they could go and stay, then get up in the mornin' and do their detail. We had maids come through and clean up the houses. We had about five of them houses in the city.

Then before you knew it, Butch started being accused of a lot a murders an' shit but they never proved that Butch did anything 'cause a lot of them murders stemmed from renegade crews like Pony Down and the Adidas Crew. I'm tellin' you, back then, he got the weight for everything.

Chapter 10

A-Team

Interviewer	Were the Pony Down and the Adidas crews part of the Y.B.I. and then branched out or were they just wanna' be's that wanted a name like Y.B.I.?
Rickey	Right, they were wanna' be's. They wanted to imitate something we did.
Interviewer	They wanted their army to be as big as the Young Boys Incorporated. They were Hip Hop followers.
Rickey	That's exactly what they were. They could never do none of the things we did. See back then, Y.B.I. had a good name and people preferred to use Y.B.I. People

would overlook those other names just to get to P. Funk, Raw Dog, Murder One, Hoochie Con or that Dyno. That dope sold itself, 'cause it had the Young Boys blessin' on it and a lot of drug addicts knew that anything they got from Y.B.I. was gone be good, top grade shit.

Interviewer So, he didn't believe in bullshittin' nobody.

Rickey No way.

Interviewer Did it come a time when stock workers would go in the pack and hit the dope or anything like that?

Rickey Naw, it was straight up law and order. If you got caught tamperin' with the packs or anything like that it probably would've cost you your life. Because all you had to do was be a clean-cut Young Boy. People would ride down the street lookin' for that image, 'cause they knew what was up.

Interviewer So, he had all his boys clean cut.

Rickey Yep.

Interviewer They had the Adidas on. You couldn't get up on no mothafuckin' Adidas unless you were rollin' back then. Adidas and Max Julian were the signs.

Rickey	Yeah people couldn't afford no Max Julians back then.
Interviewer	Hell yeah. That fifty dollars seemed more like five hundred back then.
Rickey	When you saw that, you knew that was a Y.B.I. Dope fiends knew what to look for.
Interviewer	And what about the Top Tens, especially the patent leather ones. Didn't you have to have rank if you wore the patent leather Tens. You were a lieutenant then, right.
Rickey	That's correct. It was the same way as the army, we had our colors.
Interviewer	So, you all stayed in red and white?
Rickey	Yeah, the majority of the time.
Interviewer	So tell me, what was your perception of the A-Team?
Rickey	The A-Team was put together when Butch went to jail. They were one of his mobs. The A-Team laid down law and order.
Interviewer	Was this the second time he went to jail?
Rickey	Yeah, the second time. When Butch went to jail he had got this older guy to watch over his family for him. The guy betrayed him and tried to rob his wife and kids but

Butch's son who wasn't even ten at the time killed the guy.

Interviewer So, little Mo Mo killed somebody at ten years old?

Rickey He didn't hold 'em up. The A team consisted pretty much of me, Portia, Velma, Kirk, Kethon, Billy, Farod, Spencer, and Charles. Billy was that guy. He was at the back door, the first one comin' out.

Interviewer So Butch was still runnin' things from jail?

Rickey That's right. They kept things in order. Then we had the wreckin' crew. The ones that kept it on the streets.

Rickey The wreckin' crew was a mothafucka', 'cause they put niggas in check on the street.

Interviewer They put mothafuckas in check. Mothafuckas who were doin' shit. Now, the wreckin' crew was the ones that went around and did the bat work with baseball bats. If a mothafucka' talked shit, the wreckin' crew would go see 'em and wreck they ass.

Rickey They'd wreck 'em up right quick.

Interviewer Mothafuckas would go do little shit and run off with little shit.

Rickey — The wreckin' crew would be lookin' for 'em, 'cause they'd have their picture and knew what streets they'd be on. Say, you would be down in the Brewster Projects and you'd run off. When the wreckin' crew would see you, nothin' but bats would come wreckin' at yo' ass.

Rickey — Pimpin' D. almost got it by the A-Team. Pimpin' D. and his girl Betty had a connect up in New York. Anyway Butch was lookin' for connects, 'cause he wasn't gettin' the grade of dope that he wanted. He was coppin' from everybody. Betty had connects for some good shit and like I said Pimpin' D. was her man at the time. Anyway Butch got down with Betty and pushed Pimpin' D. out the picture. He bought the girl a Cadilliac and put ten soldiers out in front of her house. He said that D. had better not come within a ten block radius. And he didn't.

Chapter 11

The Crew

Writer	Did you go to Cedar Point with them that time with those Vette's an' shit?
Rickey	Yea, I went. It was an entourage.
Writer	About how many cars was in the entourage?
Rickey	About thirty or forty. That's just the Vettes. That wasn't countin' the other cars. It was about eighty in the entourage. That's how we were ridin'. We were like a parade goin' down to Cedar Point.
Writer	Doin' a hundred and didn't get pulled over.

Rickey	Clownin'.
Interviewer	Ya'll didn't get pulled over?
Rickey	Nope.
Writer	I guess they got on the phone and was like "The Young Boys are goin' ta' Cedar Point. Don't pull 'em over. We're doing surveillance."
Rickey	Butch knew they were watchin' us.
Rickey	I remember a time when Butch had went out of the country and the spots had fell down to about five or six thousand dollars a day. The captains decided to lay me off. He was outta' the country or somewhere. Well, when he came back ta' town and found out that they had laid me off, he pitched a bitch. He told Timmy, "I betcha' this, I'm gone put Rickey back on the corner and in ten days he'll have this business back ta' twenty thousand a day." I don't know if he and Timmy bet or not. I was starvin'. I wasn't makin' any money. I had a crew down there and we were just barely makin' it.
Writer	Why did they lay you off?
Rickey	'Cause they were player haters. That first string, Richie Rich, Kirk and 'em were

jealous. I mean I had messed up some money at one time but I still knew what I was doin'. They were wrong, I mean, punish me and move on. It had been about ten thousand. It wasn't like I had stolen it, I had merely taken about ten thousand and paid my crew. I had did something they didn't want me ta' do.

So, when Butch came back and got me, he betted them that I would pick the business back up 'cause the business had dropped on Dexter. Well, after Butch came and got me, about on the sixth day I came with a Kotex box full of money. Butch said, "How much is that?" I said, "Nineteen thousand." He said, "That's nineteen off Dexter." I said, "Yeah. I done hired everybody that they fired and put 'em back ta' work".

See, I would make work for people. I would pay the lookout people everytime we'd go and get some more bundles. I would tell them, "Ya'll, give 'em a dollar." Just for the lookout people to say, "Hook. Hook comin' from Dexter. Hook comin' from off of Joy Road. Hook comin' from Davison."

Everytime you had to hurry up and get

you a bundle, we'd give 'em a dollar. At the end of the day, they would have made one hundred dollars just from hollerin', "The hook." I would create ways for people to make money. That's why people didn't mind workin' with me.

See when you sellin' dope up and down the streets, you got to be marketin'.

For example; you got a lot of people who talk to dope fiends any kinda' way. You can't do that, especially when you sellin' their product.

Writer — So, what do you think of all the Young Boys? Do you think if everybody could, they would do it again?

Do you think that there will ever be a drug crew as strong as the Young Boys?

Rickey — Naw. But I know some crews out there now clockin' twelve or thirteen thousand a day.

Interviewer — Yeah, but your talkin' about thirteen thousand versus one hundred thousand.

Writer — A big difference.

Interviewer — What about the army fatigues? Some people said that some of the Young Boys used to wear army fatigues. Was that the A-Team?

Rickey That was the wreckin' crew in the army fatigues. They would jump out in the army fatigues when they were first establishin' the law, 'cause it was certain corners that the older guys were tellin' us we couldn't roll on. So, we had to show 'em that we were gone roll there.

Writer They dressed up in army gear and went to work, with combat boots and all that shit.

Rickey The medallions and the forty-fives.

Writer They used to say that once you were in the Y.B.I. you could never get out. Was that statement true?

Rickey Not really, in the heart yeah. But some people grew out the Young Boy's. You know wanted to go legit.

Writer So the way I hear it was that each lieutenant was considered the head of a family was that right.

Rickey Right, it was about six or seven different families with different ranks.

Writer When you say families, do you mean divisions of the city?

Rickey Yeah, the overall different capitols of the city.

Writer So, the east side would be considered a

	family, the west side a family, southwest Detroit another family, you know.
Writer	You didn't make it out to Hamtramack did you?
Rickey	Naw, we didn't branch off that far.
Interviewer	So, the organization lasted from 1980 till when?
Rickey	Longer than anybody would like to admit. That's how long.
Writer	You know dope preserves them dope fiends. A lot of 'em look real good. Unlike them crackheads.
Rickey	Those crackheads, man now that's some shit, plus it's wild as hell out there with those crack niggas killin' each other, it's wild.
Writer	Exactly how many Y.B.I.s would you say were really Young Boys Incorporated, besides the wanna' be's and the renegades? How many people would you say the organization consisted of?
Rickey	I'd say maybe fifty strong.
Interviewer	Did that include the runners?
Rickey	No, that was just the family.
Writer	In the family it was fifty of the lieutenants and generals.

Rickey	Yeah.
Writer	How many employees did the Young Boys have?
Rickey	Shit, as the family grew I'd say about one thousand from east to west.
Writer	A thousand people.
Rickey	You gotta look at it like this, everyday something happened to somebody. We had groups and groups. As fast as the police was knockin' niggas is as fast as niggas were comin', wantin' to be Young Boys.
Interviewer	Did you guys initiate in order to be a Young Boy?
Rickey	Naw.
Interviewer	So, you were just welcomed in?
Writer	It's like Butch said, you had to be like a 'Bebe' kid, flat out. He didn't base his organization on kids, well some of the family members might've, but didn't no mothafuckin' straight 'A' student just drop out of school and join the organization. It was tough kids out there.
Rickey	He sent some of the guys off to college. Man Butch had big plans. It wouldn't be a lot of people out there doin' what their

For Tony, dope spells s-u-c-c-e-s-s

By Gene Schabath
News Staff Writer

The brother he respected most died of a drug overdose.

But neither that experience nor repeated dealings with Detroit's juvenile justice system — starting when he was 11 — deterred Antonio Cromer from selling heroin on street corners for Young Boys Inc

Three weeks after he was released from probation this January, because authorities said he was rehabilitated, Cromer was arrested for the second time in his young life for selling heroin.

Cromer, one of 14 children of a poor west side family, never showed for his court hearing and now is wanted by Detroit police.

The case of Antonio Angelo Cromer raises many questions, including:

WHY DID Cromer get off so lightly for four felonies, including sale and possession of heroin, which he committed as a juvenile? Why did he go back to selling drugs on the streets only

Continued on Page 6A

ANTONIO CROMER

WANTED

Detroit police rap sheet for Antonio Cromer

Date	Case action	Disposition
Feb. 10, 1976	Arrested for unarmed robbery; age 11.	Warned and released by police.
Nov. 11, 1978	Arrested for burglary; age 13.	Warned and released by police.
Nov. 5, 1980	Arrested for armed robbery.	Convicted Jan. 19, 1981, sentenced to 29 days in youth home.
May 4, 1981	Arrested for possession of 51 packets of heroin; age 16.	Convicted Aug. 11, 1981, sentenced to probation and 20 hours community service.
Jan. 5, 1982	Released from probation because he reached age 17 and because juvenile court officials wrote he "had reached a satisfactory adjustment and is no longer a problem."	
Jan. 27, 1982	Arrested as a disorderly person and for loitering; age 17.	Case pending.
Jan. 29, 1982	Arrested for sale of heroin; age 17.	Failed to show for court hearing. Fugitive at large.

For Tony Cromer, selling dope spells s-u-c-c-e-s-s

Continued from Page 1A

weeks after he had been declared by juvenile authorities to have made "a satisfactory adjustment and was no longer a problem?"

By all accounts, Cromer had a difficult life as the second youngest of 14 children, growing up around Grand River and Livernois.

The neighborhood is the heart of operations for Young Boys Inc., a Detroit teen heroin network which uses boys as young as eight to peddle hard drugs.

Cromer's mother, Mrs. Nettie White, raised the children on her own after her husband died in 1962 — two years before Cromer was born. She remarried in 1978 but is now separated from her second husband.

"He's a pretty nice, decent kid," said his mother. "He didn't give me much trouble as a youngster."

CROMER NEVER did well in school. The probation report gives this explanation:

"Antonio is a physically mature but mentally immature 16-year-old adolescent who is functioning within the borderline range of intelligence. His overall intellectual functioning is equivalent to the average 9-year-old."

Psychologists who examined Cromer added: "Antonio is a rigid and constricted youngster who is tense and anxious. He is poorly socialized, easily confused and his judgment is poor. Antonio has a strong need to please others and would be easily influenced and led. He controls his impulses through constriction and withdrawal."

Cromer's mother said her son had another jarring experience in 1976 when his older brother, Kessel, died of a drug overdose.

THAT WAS also the year that Cromer, then 11, had the first of his six arrests. He was charged with unarmed robbery, warned by police and sent home — break No. 1 for Cromer.

On Nov. 11, 1978, Cromer, then 13, was arrested for burglary. Again, he was warned by police and released. At this point, Cromer had no record with Juvenile Court because police never recommended that he be charged.

By the time Cromer was 15 he was convicted of armed robbery and sentenced to 29 days in the Wayne County Youth Home.

That was the only "jail" sentence Cromer ever served.

Two months later, police watched Cromer make several drug sales while standing around Grand River and Edmonton. When they arrested him, they found $436 in cash in his pockets and 51 packs of heroin stashed in a rubber boot he was holding.

THE HEROIN, according to police, linked Cromer to Young Boys Inc. because of the distinctive markings on the packets.

At the time, Juvenile Court Judge Thomas Maher denied a motion to have Cromer tried as an adult.

His mother insisted in an interview that her son was innocent.

"I sent Antonio to the cleaners to pick up some clothes and he said he found the rubber boot," said Mrs. Smith. "Antonio said he was innocent."

But police were told a different version the night of his arrest. When police called Cromer's home, a man who said he was Antonio's father claimed he had given Antonio $270 to buy a new suit. Police said they learned later that Cromer's father was deceased.

UNABLE TO post a $20,000 bond, he had to spend three months in the youth home until he was convicted and placed on one year's probation on Aug. 11, 1981.

Cromer's probation was shortened to five months because authorities were convinced he had been rehabilitated — and because he was considered an adult when he reached his 17th birthday last Dec. 10.

"We could have kept him on probation after age 17 but he appeared to have adjusted during the time (the five months of probation) we had him," said Ed O'Donnell, chief probation officer for Wayne County Juvenile Court.

Testimony from Cromer's mother and from a New Detroit official also helped convince authorities that Cromer had changed. Both said Cromer "did not cause them any problems." New Detroit got into the case because Cromer worked 20 hours for the agency "performing community services" as part of his probation sentence.

"The information we got was that he had made a satisfactory adjustment and was no longer a problem," said Prentis Edwards, registrar for Juvenile Court.

THE SOCIAL readjustment lasted all of three weeks.

On Jan. 29, Detroit narcotics officers moved in on a group of teen-agers suspected of selling drugs behind a church on the city's near west side.

One of the suspected teen-age drug dealers, all believed to be members of Young Boys Inc. because of the heroin packs' markings, was Antonio Angelo Cromer.

"There were a whole bunch of them selling behind that church," said Sgt. Arnold Wicker, a Detroit narcotics officer. "This was a new location for Young Boys Inc. We got complaints from the church and residents about the drug dealing going on there."

ONE NARCOTICS officer after another made drug purchases from the young dealers. Two officers posing as drug addicts bought two "dime" packets from Cromer, police said.

Then the narcotics agents made their move.

"I came up to him (Cromer) and identified myself as a police officer," said Sgt. Arnold Wicker. "The (deleted) took off running. I had to chase him for a quarter mile. They all scattered. We caught three or four of them."

Eighteen packets of heroin, all stamped with one of the Young Boys Inc. brand names, Who-Ie-Con, were found in Cromer's pockets.

Cromer was charged with the sale and possession of heroin and released on bond the following day.

That's the last police have seen of him.

WHAT LURED Cromer back to the street? Attempts to find Cromer proved unsuccessful. His mother said she was unaware of her son's latest arrest and she said she doesn't believe her son is employed by Young Boys Inc.

"I don't think he belongs to them," said Mrs. White. "My kids don't tell me a thing about that."

Cromer's former employer, Jerry Blaz, owner of Jerry's Pizza and Barbeque, gave one possible explanation. He told of an employe who quit his $50-$60 a week job to become a drug dealer.

"He came back flashing his 'Rado' (slang term for Cadillac), flashing his money and with a lot of broads," Blaz said.

"Instead of making $50 to $60 a week, they're making $1,000."

CROMER WORKED for Blaz for five weeks starting in April of 1980, earning between $25 and $60 a week doing cleanup work. Cromer told juvenile authorities that he worked the entire summer of 1980 for Blaz, earning $3.65 an hour."

"He was a very quiet person," Blaz said. "He was moody. He wouldn't talk, not even say 'hi' sometimes."

Cromer's mother said she didn't feel her son was rehabilitated.

"If he could have gotten some training, it might have helped. But the only way to get training is to serve time and I don't want him to serve time," she said.

Regina Shapiro, the specially appointed referree for Juvenile Court who placed Cromer on probation last August — after he was convicted of possession of heroin — agreed that Cromer needed job training.

But she pointed to the lack of programs for youths like Cromer:

"It's futile. What can you do with them? The training homes don't have room for them.

"They only want the ones who commit murder and arson. There's no room for those who sell heroin."

	doin' now if it wasn't for the Y.B.I.
Interviewer	So, what did they have to do in order to be a Y.B.I.?
Rickey	To show that they had heart, showed initiative, be able to think, and be able to take orders.
Interviewer	That's it?
Rickey	You got in where you fit in.
Writer	How did Big Boy say it? You're a product of your own environment. The odds are, if you grow up lookin' at dope fiends, you either gone be one or create one. That's just how it is.
Interviewer	Were you ever in jail?
Rickey	Yes, I did eight to twenty for Y.B.I.
Interviewer	How old were you?
Rickey	I was thirty-two when I went to jail.
Interviewer	Do you ever see some of those guys?
Rickey	That I was in jail with?
Writer	Any of the Y.B.I.'s
Rickey	Yeah, I was in jail with Kirk McGurk and Richie Rich.
Interviewer	Richie Rich is still in jail, right?
Rickey	Yeah.

Writer	Didn't Richie Rich get outta' jail.
Rickey	Yeah.
Writer	Where is he now?
Rickey	He's back in jail.
Writer	Damn!
Rickey	And Kirk McGurk got 20 to 40, I think.

Nicole visiting Butch in jail in St. Louis, Michigan

Stoney Roney's east side crew at it's best.

Butch's friend W.W. aka Wonderful Wayne

Jesse Jackson, Butch, Don King, and Raymond Peoples at Fundraiser Party

Kethon, Curt, Richie Rich and Paul Bunion
hangin' out at Babe's nightclub.

Butch's lovely wife Portia

Wayne Pittman and George. My friends over at the City Slicker shoe store.

My boy James Butler (in Ohio State shirt) and some of his homies up at Ionia Correctional Facility.

Tyson, John John, Cromer and Richie Rich.
Young Boys at their best

Tyson, Richie Rich, and Minute Man.

Johnny My Boy (Get wit' me man)

Arty Art and Moe Heart funnin' in Moe Heart's Benz.

Richie Rich, Timmie and Kurt McGurk

My man Moe Heart sittin on his Benz. A true player for real. Stay up player.

Darkie, Kethon, and Farod, hangin tough.

Timmie, Pebbles, Butch and Portia on the yacht that Mo Mo mentioned.

Betty and Butch at Diana Ross concert in Las Vegas

Butch meeting Jayne Kennedy at Fundraiser

Kurt Peoples, Butch, Timmie, Rerun and Lewis.
Lewis is the one kneeling.

Starting from top left: Kurt McGurk, Farod, Butch, Richie Rich, Stoney Roney, Supervisor's bitch ass turned informant (clappin' hands) Tyson and Arty Art

Richie Rich, Kethon, Butchie, Quick Kirk, John John, Butch, Moe Heart, One Gun, Arty Art, and Timmie.

Kurt McGurk and Cromer hangin' out at Palmer Park in Kurt's Benz.

Butch getting a visit in jail, still gettin' money.

Big Red, Herbie D and Richie Rich holdin' it down.

Sneed's brother, Lil' Moe with hands in the air,
Timmie and Snead on the way to Cedar Point.
That's Moe Moe in the background.

Stoney Roney, Butch, and Walter Meanifee at
Cedar Point.

Butch and Moe Moe

Butch Jones (1996)

Julius Justice
(Street Writer)

Chapter 12

Almost Death

Interview with Carlton (Fuji)

Carlton: I remember this time when Block beat some ex Young Boy's out some money and they ended up tryin' ta' kill us all.

He sold them a car and a house then refused to give it to them. It was about fifty thousand dollars that he took altogether. Anyway, we were on Sturtevant upstairs sleepin' in the bed and these guys came over to the crib about fifteen strong. They surrounded the house and threw a fire bomb threw the window. Maurice, whom we call 50, was sleepin' in the front room and they threw the firebomb through his window.

Everybody outside had Vietnamese type hats and masks around their faces. Man, once they got goin', they musta shot around four or five hundred times. Nothin' like that had ever been documented in Detroit like that before. I mean they just stood out there just blastin' away.

Interviewer So, where did ya'll go?

Carlton Well when me and my wife heard the blast we hit the floor. By this time, Block had rolled outta' bed and was asking me what was happenin'. I said, "Man, I don't know what the hell is goin' on." Butch and Portia was upstairs in the attic 'cause the attic was like another house. So I ran upstairs to tell them that they was shootin' and I heard Butch hollerin', "Yeah, I know." But he couldn't get down 'cause they were shootin' at all angles of the house.

In fact, our cousin Kethon was with the other faction that was tryna' assassinate us. But come to find out he didn't even know Butch was in the house. It was about fifteen or twenty of 'em. They had the house completely surrounded.

Interviewer Was this summertime?

CARLTON This was July 24 or 25 'cause it was right before my birthday on the 29th. The bullets were comin' threw the walls and everybody was screamin' and hollerin'.

For some reason, I don't panic under pressure ,but after it was all over that was another story.

Anyway smoke was everywhere. So, me, Mo Mo, my wife, Maurice, and Block crept down the steps to get air but when we got down to the end of the landin' I heard the front door blast open. They had shot the door off the hinges. That's when I turned back to everybody and said, "Hey ya'll, they at the door and they comin' in here. "Maurice who was only sixteen, my wife and Block all looked at each other like this was the end of our lives. I'll never forget that feelin'.

Interviewer How old was Mo Mo?

Carlton My wife had Mo Mo in her arms. He was small. I don't remember how old he was.

You know the only thang that saved us

was they didn't know if we had guns or what. That's what saved us.

Interviewer Did you guys have guns?

Carlton Nope. Butch did, but he was upstairs and with all that heavy smoke, there wasn't really that much he could do.

Interviewer So, ya'll were just there?

Carlton We were just there. Through the grace of God didn't nobody get killed.

Interviewer Did anybody get hurt?

Carlton Nope.The two guys that had busted in, Rhinehurst and the other guy whose name I don't remember, jumped off the porch.

That's when we crept on down into the basement. When we got down there me and Block just stood lookin' out the window and watchin' these cats reload their guns. At that point I got on the phone and called 911. You know how 911 is.

The operator asked me, "What are they doing?" I said, "What?!"

She said, "What are they doing?"

I said, "Bitch, listen can't you hear what they doin'?!" So, I hung up the phone, 'cause I was really pissed and I went back to the window and continued watchin.'

Interviewer So, they were shootin' up at the house?

Carlton Yeah, they were shootin' up. We was just watchin'and trippin'. I was like "There goes Chuck there Block." And he'd say, "Yeah, and there goes J.B." And whoever, and whoever. This went on for about twenty minutes.

Interviewer And no police came?

Carlton Nope.The fire department came. But after everybody started shootin' at them they took off.

So after we'd run up thinkin' we was saved, we ran back down into the basement. I couldn't believe it. Eventually the shooters left and we all came out. It was a trip. It wasn't until then that the cops, who by the way, had been standin' on the corner watchin' the whole thing came. But by then we were all so glad to be alive that we all just ran right past them. That was one day I'll never forget.

Chapter 13

Federal Penitentiary
(10 Years in Jail)

Ninety six days after I turned myself in to the federal authorities, I began servin' my official time. The first place I was sent was Terre Haute, Indiana. I was taken there in handcuffs, legshackles, and a green jumpsuit.

The next mornin' after I arrived, they flew me to F.C.I. Air Rental, Oklahoma. There, I was designated for F.C.I. Federal Correctional Institute in Oxford, Wisconsin where they stamped me number #114. There I stayed for about another four or five months before they would ship me to my next place, and that's also where I had to hit another nigga upside the head with a mop-ringer.

What happened was that me and some guys from

Wisconsin who was down with the Michigan crew got into it with some guys from California. So before I'd even gotten in the system good I'd found myself in lock down.

It wasn't long after that before I met this guy named Walter Cason. Me and him became real good friends. I had always heard of Walter Cason because Block use ta' talk about him a lot. Walt was also in jail for running a continual criminal enterprise. He'd originally gotten ten years for his crime spree, but before he'd left the courtroom he'd been given twenty.

What happened was he'd busted an F.B.I. agent in the face in court and knocked her out cold. Come to find out, Walt's girlfriend was an undercover F.B.I. agent and when he got ta' court and found that out, he just snapped and knocked her the fuck out. I mean Walt had been fuckin' this bitch all this time and had no idea who she was. So after knockin' her out he received an additional ten years. After all of that though, he still only ended up doing thirteen years and some months.

After they transferred me from Oxford, me and Walter stayed in touch and to this day we are real good friends.

After Oxford they sent me to El Reno for a few days and from there I got designated to Bastrop, Texas. Bastrop, Texas is an administrative joint that holds all levels, from one through four. Any penitentiary that is a level four on down is considered a Federal Correctional Institute and anythang with a level five on up is considered a penitentiary. They sent me and this guy named Earl there. All I gotta say about Bastrop is, if I'd been able ta' do my whole stay there, I would not have had a complaint in the world. At Bastrop it was one man to a room. Everywhere else had been two men to a room.

Anyway, I loved the place. For the three years that I was there, it seemed like there wasn't a day that the sun didn't shine or we didn't have eighty degree weather.

While I was in Bastrop, Not only was the whether perfect, but I even got so lucky as to start gettin' pussy from one of the guards..

What happened was the correctional officer had been in the service before she'd gotten the job at Bastrop and while in the service her daughter had ended up gettin' burned by mistake, while in the hands of a babysitter. Anyway to make a long story short, she got discharged from the army and moved to Texas, 'cause they had a burn center in Texas.

Now what led me to her, was that while at Bastrop, I'd taken up several trades. One of the trades I took up was auto-mechanics, which they gave me some credits from a college in Austin, Texas. I was kinda' proud of that. I also took up buildin' maintenance, or janitorial work and I also participated in several counseling groups and several impulse control groups, whose purpose was to help with temper and anger control and things like that.

Anyway out of all of that, I ended up gettin' a job as the janitor in unit one. They didn't actually call the job *janitor* they called it a *porter* but it was all the same. Anyway as a janitor, one of my details was to clean the showers. They didn't have community bathrooms in Bastrop, 'cause each room had it's own toilet. That was good, 'cause it gave you privacy. Well, this correctional officer who I was tellin' you about, while I would be doin' my work we would be holdin' discussions. Not really about nothin' much, but enough where she ended up tellin' me about her daughter.

So, one day I told her that I wanted to get a P.O. box because I was interested in helpin' her daughter. She was kinda leery, but she ended up gettin' the P.O. box for me. I then told her I would send her daughter five hundred dollars and when she got it not to worry about it.

I told her that everythang that was did for me, was did from Detroit, cause I didn't have nobody in Texas so they would be sendin' it from there. But you know how people are, I guess she thought I was playin' 'cause I could tell that she didn't take me serious.

After about a week however, she got the money order and from that day on she was never the same. She came to me all excited. She was like, "I got that money order. I don't know how to repay you." I said, "Look, this is not for you, it's for your daughter. Don't worry about repayin' it. It's just to help on some of the bills that's all." I really did understand because I knew that she only got paid every two weeks and so like any friend, if I could help, I did. And so I did.

Anyway, when she found out I was a stand-up guy, and that she didn't have to worry about nothin' bein' repeated that we talked about, we became good friends. But you know how it is, I'm a guy and she's a girl, so it was only a matter of time before I would have ta' crack on the pussy, you know.

So, one day, I just broke and asked her, "Is it alright if I talk to you without drawin' lines on my conversation?"

And she said, "What do you mean?"

I said, "Well, I don't wanna' say nothin', then you get offended and write me a ticket and get me in trouble, you know."

But she was like, "Naw, you don't have to draw any lines in your conversation with me."

So, I said, "I wanna' talk to you like a man talks to a woman. I got eyes for you."

She said, "What do you mean?"

I said, "I kinda like you. You ain't offended by me sayin' this are you?"

And she told me, "No."

Nothin' really happened for the first few months or so, but I did began to slowly but surely talk to her the way a man would talk to a woman. You know, tell her how good she looked, how pretty she smelled. You know lil' stuff like that. So one day after I couldn't take it any longer I just told her, "Look, I been locked up for what seems like forever and I need some pussy baby, I wanna' fuck." I didn't really know how she would respond, but at that point all I knew was I wanted some pussy and if I was gonna get some, I had no choice but to say what I said.

Come ta' find out, I'd said the right thing 'cause before you knew it we was in the supply room fuckin' like wild dogs. And from that day on, whenever we would get the chance we would fuck.

The thang that turned me on the most, was that I was fuckin' a uniformed correctional officer.

Man, when I was in Bastrop I didn't even know I was in jail 'cause not only was I gettin' pussy, I was also gettin' money.

I had put together this football pool, whereas I would charge each person a dollar ta' pick a square, with the choice of total squares being one hundred. A football game has four quarters, so the way it was set up was whatever the score was at the end of the quarter then the person who picked that number would win twenty dollars. Like I said, whenever somebody would win on a quarter, I would pay 'em twenty dollars. Each game I would take in one hundred dollars total and pay out eighty. I would make a quick twenty dollar profit and in jail twenty dollars a day adds up.

I also sold marijuana. I sold three joints for ten dollars and that went pretty good.

In terms of the weed, I had a one hundred percent markup 'cause I was gettin' the weed for free.

Then on top of that, I was loanin' money. Two for one. If somebody borrowed ten dollars from me, then they would have to pay me twenty dollars back.

And last but not least, I had a store. Like I said, it was all a hustle while I was in Bastrap, 'cause everythang was gravy. I was the only person there from Detroit, so I was way more advanced than the rest of the guys. That's the way I seen it.

To tell you the truth, it was really a proud time for me, because when my wife would come to see me, I would have fifteen hundred ta' twenty-five hundred dollars. I would give her the money and she would take it back to Detroit.

Also because of my hustles I would recieve a lot of change. So I had another guard that would take the change out of the prison for me, and turn it into green money. For that, I would let her keep a small portion for herself. If I gave her one hundred dollars in change, then she would keep twenty-five, and give me seventy-five. If I sent her out with one hundred and fifty dollars worth a change, then she would bring me a hundred dollar bill and keep fifty. That's how I was turnin' the change into green money.

I would have this same guard to mark down in the book that she had searched my cell, so when the afternoon shift came, I didn't have ta' worry about them searchin' my room. So that's how I was able to keep all the contraband in my room.

In terms of the weed, this guy named Oscar who worked over in auto mechanics was the one who would bring me that. He wasn't a correctional officer, he was a civilian who came in ta' teach a college class. He was gettin' paid from the college in Austin, Texas and what made him cool was that he didn't really care too much for the government, so he didn't have no problem with bringin' the stuff in for me.

Man, for awhile, I was doin' so well in Bastrop that I was able to pay my own prison phone bills. My phone bill was 'eighteen hundred dollars a month.

After some time of livin' this great life in prison, one Saturday, my change connection fucked up and got caught. Another officer, a lieutenant, asked her where she got all the change from and she told him that the change was hers. But he took it from her and called the F.B.I., 'cause everythang that happens in federal prison the F.B.I. has to investigate .

So, they interrogated her for about ten hours tryna' get her to tell where she got the change from. Some kinda way my name came up and they came and put me up in segregation.

I knew all along that she hadn't told, 'cause each night she would call and let my mother know what was goin' on. So, when I got on the phone I would call my mother and she would let me know what was goin' on. So when they came back tellin' me that she had told on me and for me to tell about my involvement, I already knew that they didn't have nothin'. It was the same old game that they were tryin' ta' play-the good agent/bad agent. I didn't have nothin' ta' say, 'cause I never make a statement no matter how bad it seems. Never.

After I stayed in segregation for about thirty days, they decided I was guilty and that Bastrop was not the prison for me, so they fired the guard and then sent me to one of the worst and oldest prisons in the United States: Leavenworth.

When I arrived at Leavenworth I looked around and realized that life would never be the same.

When we pulled up, it looked real scary, I mean this joint looked like a replica of the White House with a bunch of bars and gates, so I knew that anythang that looked that much like government meant business. The place had all these stairs you had ta' walk up, and with handcuffs and shackles holdin' you down, it seemed like the longest walk of my life. They had sent me to Leavenworth for the crime of corruptin' an officer. They didn't know how many other officers I had corrupted, 'cause all the staff liked me. So for that, I got Leavenworth prison.

Through all my years in prison and on the streets, I had heard stories about Leavenworth and knew the criteria ta' get in. The criteria was twenty years ta' life.

Now I remind you, I was doin' twelve years with no parole and had already did four. So, technically Leavenworth was not suppose to even accept me, but the government got them to accept me on the strength that I had corrupted an officer.

Anyway, before I proceed just let me tell you about the bus ride there. You ain't been on a bus ride until you ride on a bus headed to one of the toughest prisons in the world. First of all, you're on this bus and everybody on it is lookin' at the other person like the first thang you say ta' me I'mo kill yo' mothafucken ass.

The majority of the guys on the bus were comin' from Marian, which is considered the highest level, toughest U.S. Prison in the world.

At Marian, they only let you out of your cell for one hour a day, for the rest of your life.

So wasn't nobody talkin' ta' nobody, 'cause these guys were just plain hard. Everybody had life sentences and didn't nobody give a fuck about nothin'. If the other inmates would have found out that I was in that prison with just several years left on my sentence, I would have gotten killed just based on that fact.

Anyway once we got inside, they unchained me and I quickly changed my clothes. After that, they gave me my room.

The first thang I did was call my mother to let her know where the government had sent me.

Like I said, while at Bastrop they had held me in segregation for thirty days, so I had not been able ta' use the phone durin' the entire time. So when I got a chance to call my mother that was a big relief 'cause I felt a conspiracy was goin' on, 'cause I wasn't even suppose ta' be in Leavenworth. And that's what I told her. I also told her that I needed money to buy me a knife so I could protect myself, 'cause I already knew that stabbings and killings went on in Leavenworth everyday. It's a way of life.

I then told her, "Mama, they done sent me to Leavenworth for one of two reasons. For me to kill somebody or for somebody to kill me. Either way it goes, the government wins." I felt like I was in a no-win situation.

The next day, I found somebody to make me a knife. It was a boy outta' Kansas City who charged me fifty dollars. I told him I was gone have my people to send me the money through the Western Union, and he gave me a name to which to send the money to.

When he got the money he gave me the knife. It was like an ice pick with grey tape around it. It was a real firm, nice ice pick. You could really do some stabbin' with it. I liked the way it felt and everywhere I went I kept that ice pick on me. Although they search you periodically in Leavenworth, I didn't feel like I was gone be searched, 'cause I had just gotten there and I didn't know anybody.

At most, all they ever seen me do was play a lil' chess.

I had started playin' chess with this guy named Sweets, who was outta' D.C. Sweets was doin' thirty to sixty. He had also been in Marian and had gotten there the same day I had. I had let him know that I had got a knife and if he needed me to watch his back or anything I would, 'cause I took a likin' ta' him and he'd also taken a likin' ta' me. Me and him became best friends while I was there.

During the first month at Leavenworth, everybody

gets a review. They tell you why you're there and what's expected of you. When I went to see the captain for my review, they said, "Damn, you're not really doin' enough time to really be in Leavenworth," and I said, "That's what I'm sayin' Captain. I shouldn't even be here." So, he told me to give him a month to find out why I was bein' sent ta' Leavenworth, then he'd get back with me.

After the month went by, he called me back down to his office and told me I was gone have to be there for at least six months, and then he would be able ta' transfer me outta' there. He told me to give him clear conduct, don't get in no trouble, hurt nobody, or anythang like that and he would transfer me outta' there. So the first six months, all I did was watch my back, play bridge, play chess, and cross train.

When the six months was up and I had my review, the Captain told me that he still couldn't send me nowhere, 'cause I was an administrative prisoner. That I had an 848, and Washington had all the say so over me, in terms of whether I went here or there. And that only when D.C. gave the nod for me ta' get transferred would I be able ta' leave. So, I asked him to get in touch with the Bureau of Prisons in Washington to see if I could get transferred and he told me that he would.

After one year had gone by they still hadn't transferred me and in that time span, about eighteen people had gotten killed. I saw two stabbings myself. One stabbin' happened while I was in the movies.

Everybody was just sittin' there, then all a sudden

this guy grabbed this dude's head with one hand and Bam! stuck the knife right through the chair into his back, and kept stabbin' him.

The other stabbin' happened right in the hallway near the store. Now, anybody that's been ta' Leavenworth knows that the store is right there in the rotunda and the captain's office is on the right hand side of the hallway. But in a place like this, people don't give a fuck.

Now what happened this time was a guy took cuts goin' to the store, and this Cuban guy went off and stabbed this guy right there in the hallway and killed him. Like I said, I had already heard stories and knew this was a serious place. Everythang that you got into in this place was real serious and thangs like takin' cuts could cost you your life.

After I had been there a year, I got into my first incident. I was workin' in the kitchen 'cause I had requested a kitchen detail job so I could stay around those knives.

Anyway, this guy who was assigned to work in the back with me decided that he didn't want ta' do his part and I guess he called himself gone get frustrated and try an' take it out on me. Our job was to bring the produce out and make the salads and everythang. So, guy tells me, "I ain't doin' none of this shit today. You gone have to do everything."

And I said, "All I'm gone do is my part. Whatever you don't wanna' do is on you. You take it up with the supervisor."

And he said, "Well, if I don't do my work are you gonna tell on me?"

I said, "Man, I don't know you. I ain't got nothin' ta' say. I ain't tellin' on nobody. All I'm gone do is what I'm suppose ta' do. When I get done, I'm goin' back to my my cell. It's as simple as that. I ain't got nothin' ta' do with whatever you do."

I did just that. I did my detail and left.

So, the next day guy tells me that he got in trouble 'cause of what he didn't do that I was suppose ta' do.

I said, "I already told you I ain't doin' yo' work. That's on you. If you don't wanna' work in the kitchen, tell the people and get reassigned. Do whatever you gotta do, but leave me the fuck alone."

Man, the guy comes back there, I guess he must had been drankin' some of that spud whiskey they make, and tried ta' swing on me. So I moved back, then he swung on me again. This time I went on and picked him up, slammed him to the floor, stomped him, and knocked him out.

The next day, some kinda way this guy gets a knife and word comes back to me that this guy is gone stab me. Now, I had to stab this guy or he was gonna stab me. I done got put in somethin' that really I didn't have nothin' ta' do with, 'cause if he didn't wanna' work in the kitchen he should've told 'em.

Anyway as soon as he came to work, I waited for him to come back where we worked, which was behind some cages, and I went on and did what I had to do. I stabbed the shit outta' the punk ass bitch.

When he went to the hospital, they came and got me and asked me what happened and I said, "I didn't know what happened. He must've came back there stabbed." So they locked me down again and this time I stayed under investigation for sixty days. The guy didn't tell on me though, so I got back out. From there, I figured that everythang was cool.

After that, and being bored of not makin' any money, I got the guy that had gotten me the knife to cooperate with me on this heroin hookup. All I had ta' do was get the heroin sent ta' him and he would bring it in for a third of the take. If I got three grams then I got to keep two grams and he got a gram for bringin' it in. So before you knew it, I was sellin' heroin at five hundred dollars a gram.

The guys from D.C. didn't like what I was doin', because they had this geographical thang that if you from Detroit then they don't like you. They called us bamas. Everybody from Detroit had ta' be a bama.

I didn't care what a mothafucka called me, just don't call me late for chow or late for goin' home. That's the way I looked at it. I wasn't really gone hurt nobody about nothin' they said, as long as a mothafucka didn't call me no dick sucker, snitch, or nothin' like that. I didn't really play the name callin' game with nobody.

I didn't get that personal where a mothafucka called me a dick sucker or a bitch, 'cause I'm like this, if you done called me outta' my name to that extent, you got somethin' else on your mind, and it's goin' down then. That's the way I looked at it. I'm like that today. If a person calls me a bitch, dick sucker, snitch or any of that shit then it's goin' down. I'm gonna' hurt somebody and it ain't no two or three ways about it.

After I'd got fired from the kitchen, I got an orderly job workin' on the fifth tier.

In Leavenworth they have this one block with five tiers, or floors. Then it has another block with single cells for people who can't cell with nobody. In other words, they have to be by themselves.

Anyway, my job was now to work the fifth tier. The way I played it was I would always keep my knife in the mop bucket with the water in the bucket, so if I had to go through anywhere I could just push my mop bucket with me. I took my mop bucket with me everywhere, 'cause all I had ta' do was reach in my bucket and there was my knife. Everythang I did, I did on that floor, 'cause that's where I stayed. They had card rooms on every floor but I watched tv and played cards on the fifth gallery.

So, one day I was playin' pinochle with this Indian boy name High Walker. High Walker was my pinochle partner. We were playin against two older Italian guys in their sixties when these three dudes from D.C. came into the card room.

"Hey, we gotta have that table," they said.

Now, it was three other tables in this card room, but they wanted this particular table that we were playin' on.

The two Italian guys immediately got up, 'cause they were older and didn't want no trouble. Like I said the three guys were from D.C. and nobody really wanted any trouble with them, 'cause when you get into a beef with guys from D.C. it's thirty or forty of 'em that you have to fight. They're homeboys and stick together like that. The majority of 'em are in the Mooris Temple, they're Moors.

So, I looked at these guys and I also didn't want no problems, 'cause I was readin' the play. I felt like they were really comin' in there ta' do me, 'cause I was sellin' this raw and I hadn't givin' nobody no cut, especially nobody from D.C., 'cause only a few of them had money anyway.

So, the mothafucka asked me, "You gotta problem about givin' this table up?"

And I just looked at him, you know. I swallowed my pride and put a smile on my face 'cause I saw that they were tryna' bait me into somethin' and like I said, I was readin' the play.

So I said, "Naw man, I ain't got no problem about the table. Ya'll can have this table. I know ya'll wanna' shoot some dice."

I then put the cards back in the box and went ta' pick up my blanket but because they proceeded to surround me I went on and got up and left the blanket on the table and walked on out.

High Walker had already gotten up and left the card room.

When I got back to my cell, I was pissed. I told Vick, my cellmate and chess partner, who ironically, was also from Detroit that it was time for them mothafuckas to die. I told him what they had done in the cardroom and that now it was time for me ta' make the next move.

I started packin' my shit, 'cause I knew I was goin' to the hole in the mornin'. This was something I was not about to swallow. Deep down inside I really didn't wanna' do what I had ta' do, but they'd left me no choice. I had ta' do what I had ta' do.

So, I packed all my shit that night, put on the clothes I would wear and began to plot my moves. I couldn't sleep 'cause like all the times in the past, whenever I would get ready to go on a mission my heart would just get ta' beatin' thus not allowin' me ta' sleep. Plus I had to go over everythang in my head to make sure that I had everythang down pack? What could go wrong? What could be the consequences? How I would get back to my cell?

Finally 6:00 a.m. arrived and I listened for the guard to make the last count. When he makes the last count that's when they break the doors, but when they break the doors, a lot of people are still lyin' in their bunks sleep. So I jumped up.

Now Dave and Kevin, the two dudes that had surrounded me stayed down on three so I headed on down. As soon as they broke the third floor, I was right there at their door. I eased right in without them hearin' a sound. Dave was on the top bunk and Kevin was on the bottom bunk. So, I tapped Dave first.

"Dave, hey Dave, wake up," I said. "I wanna' talk to you about that table, man."

He looked up and seen me in that dark room and he damn near shitted. I had the icepick in my hand and after he got his focus, he saw it, and that's when he panicked.

By this time, Kevin had got up and was tryna' rush me. So, I stuck Kevin twice. Yak. Yak. The first one hit him once in the hand and the second one got 'em in his ass. That's because after I cut 'him the first time he took off runnin'. So I stuck him in the ass on his way out the door.

Then I turned around and gave Dave all my attention, 'cause while I was givin it to his boy, he was tryna' position himself ta' jump off the top bunk without gettin' stabbed on his way down. But by the time he got down, I'd stuck him three or four times.

Now mind you, before I'd walked into that room I had been somewhat convinced that this was a real tough guy, 'cause he always walked around with his face tore-up and he always had a lot of back up. Plus he had a reputation for knockin' all yo' teeth outta' yo' mouth. To tell you the truth, I was scared of him.

Anyway as I was hittin' this mothafucka' with the icepick, and blockin' him from runnin' out the cell, all a sudden this mothafucka' just gets ta' hollerin', "Ahh! Ahh! Somebody help!"

Man, he woke up everybody in the block. I

would've never suspected that this guy woulda' went ta' hollerin', 'cause I knew if I woulda' got stabbed I woulda' taken it like a man. That's the way I had always seen it.

Man, this mothafucka' got up outta' that room hollerin' like a bitch.

He was runnin' down the stairway hollerin, "Ahhh!Ahhh!Ahhh! Get him! I'm stabbed! Get him!"

After he ran on outta' there, I eased on out the cell and ran back to the fifth floor. Because I had blood all over me, I ran to the laundry room and stripped my clothes off. I had already tore my number outta' the pants and shirt, so I took the clothes and put them in the washer and started it. Then went back to my cell with my underwear on.

By this time, they had hit the alarm and was hollerin'. "Lockup!"

After I got back to my cell I ran into it and then walked back out in my underwear like I'd been in my cell the whole time.

Because they were hollerin' lockup, I went on and walked back into my cell.

Suddenly I heard the police runnin' upstairs with their keys jinglin'. My adrenaline was still pumpin' and I was tryna' calm down, but I couldn't, 'cause I hadn't had enough time to relax.

When they came up on my floor, they made me and Vick step out on the gallery so they could shake down our room. They asked me did I see anythang and I said no. Then they asked Vick the same question and he said no.

Then the guy looked at me kinda' funny. He turned away like he was gone walk out the cell, then he quickly turned back around, stuck his hand up to my heart, and asked me why my heart was beaten so fast.

Man, I'm tellin' you, my heart was about to jump outta' my chest. Anyway, my reply was that they had woke me up, and blah, blah, blah, and my man was like yea, yea, convict. He then checked Vick's heart to see if his heart was beatin' fast, but it wasn't, so they took me down to the lieutenants office.

After I got downstairs they played the camera, which they had on each floor, to see if that was me who'd entered Dave and Kevin's room.

But all you could see was somebody with some whites on. You couldn't really see my face. You saw a figure go in the room and about two or three minutes later you saw Kevin run outta' the room, and about two or three minutes after that you saw Dave runnin' outta' the room with his hands up hollerin' an' shit. Then you see the guy with the whites on run outta' the room real smooth, stayin' close to the wall and then disappear upstairs.

Anyway, after a few more questions they put me under investigation and then sent me down to segregation.

About two days later, the F.B.I. came to see me and told me that they had kites on me. Kites is when inmates write into the lieutenants office and tell all your business. They tell everythang in Leavenworth. As a matter of fact, you got some of the most tellin'est mothafuckas in the world at Levensworth, 'cause everybody tellin' ta' try ta' get outta' the joint.

So, I told the F.B.I., as usual, "I don't got nothin' ta' say. I don't know what's goin' on. Why ya'll got me in the hole? Why everytime somethin' happens ya'll lock me up and blame it on me? It's a conspiracy." They were like yea, yea, they were gonna' prosecute me but in the mean time they were gonna' let me outta' segregation and let me go back to my cell.

After I got back out to population, I got a wire that when I got back out to the yard, that Dave and Kevin was gone kill me.

But by then I was like, yea right. Them bitches ain't gone do a mothafuckin' thang, but holler an' scream just like they did the first time. If any mothafucka' fucks with me, then they're gone get the same thang that Dave got.

I was just relieved that they hadn't told on me and I knew they wouldn't because they were too busy talkin' about what they were gonna' do.

Dave really did wanna' kill me, 'cause he was mad that somebody had gotten the nerve ta' try him. So I guess he figured with all the friends he had in prison with him, it was only a matter of time before they'd get me.

What ended up happenin' was after about ninety days, thanks to Otis Culpepper, Paul Curtis and Dominique Serease, I was given' an administrative transfer to

Phoenix, Arizona. 'I had called Otis and told him to put some pressure from Detroit on the system because I knew if I stayed there too much longer, that I was either gonna' have ta' kill somebody or be killed. So, they got me outta' Leavenworth, and for that, I am very grateful.

They sent Dave to Terre Haute and Kevin to Kentucky. They split us all up. Once they split you up in a federal system you never see the person again, 'cause that's how they do it. They say that you got a sponge and what that means is that you're on separation. I was on separation from them and they were on separation from me. I never saw them again.

Guys that came from Terre Haute would always tell stories about how I'd stabbed Dave and how he'd tried to fight me back and I would always say to myself, yea right.

Anyway, after I got to Arizona the guys from D.C. told me that they didn't really want no trouble with me and that whatever happened in Leavenworth happened in Leavenworth. That's the way they looked at it.

What I really felt that they were sayin' was, that if I had enough heart to stab Dave, then I really wouldn't have no problem stabbin' their asses. And they were right. I was lookin' at self preservation and I wasn't lettin' nothin' happen ta' me.

After I got there, I did my regular thang. I got myself a porters job and continued to cross train. At this time, I was runnin' ten miles every other day. Plus I walked five miles a day, played racketball and basketball, punched the punchin' bag, and bench pressed three hundred and fifteen pounds. So, I was in shape. My weight would fluctuate from two hundred to two hundred twenty. And I was solid.

But I didn't have ta' get a knife or anything while I was there because they had the place set up like a college campus, you know. It was a real layed back place. That's basically how I did time. I did time, I didn't let time do me. I kept busy. If I wasn't exercisin' I was in the law library tryin' ta' read everythang I got my hands on. Then I would go back to my unit.

At night time, I would play chess and if I wasn't playin' chess then I gambled. Like I said, I had to keep a hustle. In Arizona, they like to play tunk with ten and five. Five dollars on the game and ten if you tunked out. Plus I would play pinochle, 'cause that was another game that everybody use ta' bet on.

Chapter 14

Epilogue

Checkmate

Out of everything I ever did in prison, the one thing I excelled at the most was chess. Everybody admired my chess game, 'cause I was the best. I could beat them all: the Russians, the Cubans, the Chinese, the white boys and anybody else I played. Anybody I played I kicked their ass. Plain and simple.

You see, I play chess just like I built Young Boy's. And that's by playing a real aggressive game and looking at my moves ahead. In this instance at least eight. At first I was playin' on an 'A' level, then I took my game up to a masters level.

Everytime I play a game, I know the first eight moves that I'm gonna' make. When I play chess, I play forced chess. In other words, I make a move and then I predict what you will move. When you move it's like choosin' the lesser of two evils, 'cause if you choose, you're gonna' lose one piece one way or two pieces another way. That's how I play chess. That way I can always predict I'm gonna win 98% of the time.

I don't care how tough my opponent is, I'm just gone play a little tougher. I play it on a real aggressive level. I can play it real fast or real slow. It doesn't matter to me as long as I win. I play ta' win. That's the main thang. So, of course, I could never really get nobody to gamble with me playin' chess, 'cause I had a reputation throughout the system as bein' a chess master. I had a real good game of pinochle, too.

As soon as I got settled at the new prison, I had me some money sent and I started loanin' money again, 'cause that's a real good hustle. I also got me a store so I could sell soup, potato chips, candy bars and thangs of that nature.

Also, while in Arizona, I got a chance to meet some good guys outta' California. I was tight with a lot of guys outta' California. They were guys that were worthy of doin' thangs, you know. '

When it came time for me to leave Arizona, I really didn't wanna' leave. I loved the weather down there, plus the staff treated me real nice. Everybody took ta' me like a fish took to water. I felt like I was in a comfort zone, a safe zone, ya' know, and I wanted to stay there. I really wanted to go home from there since I had bought me a house in Arizona and knew a whole lot about Arizona. I was just gone go ahead and relocate there. But after eight years of being in the federal system, they released me.

Instead of going home though, I had another State case which I'd been convicted of: accessory-after-the-fact, with respect to the shooting of Herman Amos. For that they sent me to Jackson, Michigan, where I stayed in the State prison system another two years.

When I went to the State joint, it was the same ol' thang. But I was really more at home, 'cause everybody was from Detroit, Flint or Pontiac and I considered them my homies, you know. After being locked up with people from different countries and shit like that I was just glad ta' be home.

When I was in the State system, I really didn't have ta' do any violence, because I rode with a lot of guys from the west side. Plus, I had friends from the east side, Pontiac, and Flint. So, everythang was real steady and smooth, ya' know. I went on and did that bit and came on home.

After I finished doin' my time, I joined the Chess Confederation. My chess I.D. number is 12578296. I'm registered in the chess books and I'm about two hundred points away from bein' a grand master. I can draw social security from playin' chess if I play it for twenty years and participate in all the chess tournaments throughout the country. I've already been to Chicago, Texas, and California to play in tournaments.

Also when I got home things changed a lot for me in terms of the way I'd been used to makin' a livin'. I got a job through a friend of mine, a deputy named Jeffrey Templeton. He and my friend Von are real good friends of mine. These are two guys that I admire and look up to. I look up to all the Wayne County Dep's., 'cause I feel like they're doin' a job just like anybody else. They just picked law enforcement.

Anyway, Temp got me this job workin' with this guy name Jimmy who owns a landscapin' business. Generally when landscapin' is mentioned you immediately underestimate the business, but I'm here ta' tell you, it's a lot of money ta' be made in that business. It ain't dope of course. But what is. Anyway he is another real nice guy that took a likin' ta' me and wanted to help me turn my life around.

You know, what I would really like ta' do is get into some of the schools and let the kids know that this society has traps set. If you look at who the most successful people in this society are, it definitely won't be people from your family. That's just the percentages.

Yea you might hear of a Black man or woman that's doing real good, or you might see the President appoint one of us and then put him or her out in front as if we really got it going on. But I guarantee that that Black person they're puttin' out in front is livin' like lost in space. Their out there alone.

I'm not saying that we can't be successful, but what I am saying is we have to be independent. Create our own jobs. Our own businesses. We must not be so quick to accept less than what we're capable of achieving.

Keep in mind, we're the natural rulers of this world. Black people. The second that you fall victim to the misconception that we can't do nothin' but sell drugs, rap a lot, or talk ourselves into a good movie is the day that we will go the way of the Indian.

If anything, that should be a lesson for us. Races of people can get annihilated. How many of you had Indians in your family and now all you have is a great grandparent's memory left to go on?

These people are not playing out here. They built this country on the backs of illegal activity and now they have no intentions of lettin' anybody else do the same thing. Trust me. We must gain our economic independence. We must!

You see how they've programmed us. Black males think it's weak to be smart. So everybody walk around like they hard, ready to kill they own brother. Brother you been tricked. What's up with that? I ain't actin' like I'm exempt. I'm caught up too. But what the fuck. It's the society I'm caught up in. Most brothers ain't gone give a fuck, so if one of them try ta' do me, I have no choice.

But that's my point. Why should we even have to go through this?

I'll tell you why. Because the system has it set up where we have to fight like dogs against each other just ta' get a damn bone. That's why.

The system is set up in such a way that the first time you commit a crime they tryna' lock you up. They tryna' get you out the way.

Then they send these subliminal messages to your woman to keep her tellin' you, you ain't shit, and neither of you understand why she disrespects you so bad. She thinks she knows the reason, but it's bigger than that simple argument you just had.

It's bigger than these Black woman on the radio and on t.v. that's been hired by the system to lead this false charade of the destruction of the Black man. You hear them everyday on the air, always puttin' us down as if we're a joke.

Black woman, it ain't all on us. It's one thang for us to fall victim to the self destructive ways of our times, but don't you be tricked. Without you it is impossible for us to ever climb out of this hole. Once we're out of the way, what do you think is gonna' happen to you. Let's learn how to read between the lines. Let's realize that just because somebody is in a position of power and makin' money, that they are not necessarily in a position to lead. Let's learn to realize when we've been tricked. Let's learn!

And last but not least, in case you think I'm just blowin' shit outta' my mouth, remember, the whole time I was clockin' I never got busted. What they did was convict me of runnin' a continual criminal enterprise. Basically, that's the same thing they're tryin' to indict the President on, but of course, he's not from the west side of Detroit. It doesn't matter. Drugs. Money scandals. A crime is a crime.

So in case you think I was stupid or that I slipped, you're wrong. I was as smooth as they come. But like I said earlier. I ain't no Kennedy. Or no Clinton. I'm a Black man from the west side, and they were intent on not allowing me to take over the political, economic and social fabric of Detroit.

And I'll tell you, had they not created a law to bring me down, that's exactly where I was headed.

Hell, somebody had to take over this city. Why not me?

Author Raymond Canty

ACKNOWLEDGMENTS

I would like to give special acknowledgments to my best friend and author of this book Raymond Canty, and to co-author Julius Justice. Without their long hours of research, editing, and support for this book, its completion could have never come about and this book would have never become a national bestseller. I would like to thank my mother, father, and my family for their support and encouragement. I also, would like to thank my wife, son and family for the encouragement and support that they gave me in continuin' to put this book together and to keep it real. I also would like to thank my friends for the love, respect and encouragement that I got from them. I would like to thank Kethon and Moe Heart. Without their love and support I would have never followed through. I would like to thank my attorneys and friends W. Otis Culpepper, Paul Curtis, Bill Hunter, Marlon B. Evans, Danny Blake, Richard Lustic, David Steingold, Sheldon Helpburn, Judge Crockett, Attorney Collins, Attorney Sam Gardner, Dominic Serease, and Bobby Kennedy which is Otis Culpepper's partner. I would like to send special shoutouts to my friends Inspector Richardson,

Commmander Gerald Stewart, Lieutenant Bill Rice, my basketball partner, Sergeant Harvel, Popeye of the Gang Squad, and Commander Whicker at the Detroit Police Department. Thanks for your support in keeping me on the right track. I would like to send a special shoutout to Mr. E. L. Thompson, who was my parole officer and gave me a lot of encouragement to stay off the street and do somethin' positive with my life. I would like to send special shoutouts to Von, Jeff Templeton, Officer Allen, my man Big Al and Commander Watts and all the rest of the Wayne County Deps. All of 'em treated me nice. I would like to thank my nephew Ceville who wasn't a trader, stayed by my side no matter what and never took sides against me-I love ya player and stay up. Special thanks to my cousins Leslie, Karen, Paula, Kethon, Steve, Marty, and Parish (Pay Pay) of the Green family. Special thanks to my cousins Najean, Antoine, Keisha, Pam, Monique, and Kenyata from my daddy's side. Special thanks to Amani Abdul for your interviews and Metri Duley for your computer expertise. Special thanks to Boo, Linda, Marty, and my stepdaughter Nicole. To Linda and Brenda on Martindale and son Michael Jr., much love and forgive me for whatever I did in the past. You know what I mean. I would like to thank Moe Heart's family who I love and respect with a special thanks to Moe Heart's sister Lacretia. Stay up player. Special thanks to my cousin Cat, my cousin Little Donald, my sister Lanette, my brothers Bay Bay, Rickey and Charlie, my Uncle Arthur, and the rest of my family. I have too many cousins to mention, but I want ya'll to know that I was thinkin' about ya'll. I just wanna' say this to all the sellouts, dick lickers who jumped ship, who didn't have no faith or loyalty to me, and talked about me behind my back-eat a fat dick. Teflon bullets to you bitches. I wanna' give special thanks to the ninth floor detention officers at 1300 Beaubien, especially Reggie B. and Mr. Moe. Special shoutouts go out to Wayne Pittman and George of City Slickers Shoe Store. Special shoutouts to Horace, his sister Betty, and all the people that I play cards with on Hubbell. Shoutouts to Prince Rankin outta' Ohio, Treacherous down in Tennessee, Ervin Davis who has the Dexter car wash. Shoutout to a real special friend of mine called Jarod Spencer (Little G.), my man off of Fenkell. I wanna' give special thanks to Ostelle, his brother Charles, D., and Fat George who is my best friend and mentor. He taught me everythang I know about gamblin' today. Special thanks to my main man Milwaukee Jack, stay up player. Special thanks to my Aunt Ruth, Uncle Sam and their family. Love and respect go out to the Townsend Family, Harrell Family, Terrell Family, and my man Black and his family.

Slim, I just wanna' say that I'm sorry about everything that happened. I'm speaking from the heart now. Man, I still love you like a brother and whenever you read this book call me, and stay strong.

I wanna' say hello to everybody that's in the State and Federal system. I can feel everythang you goin' through, 'cause I did sixteen years myself. I know how it feels to be away from home. All I'm tryna' do is somethin' that nobody in the game has ever done before. I'm tryna' break the ice not just for myself, but for everybody that's been in the game and has a story ta' tell. I'm tryna' do the groundwork now, so when somebody else does an autobiography of their life they can come to see me or my man Fat Boy. Fat Boy gone make it happen for 'em. That's the way I see it. If Fat Boy don't make it happen for 'em, I'm gone make it happen for 'em. Me and Fat Boy are C.M.B., the Cash Money Brothers. Ya'll gone be hearin' that name in town. C.M.B.!!

Stony, I just wanna' say to you, man, I want you to be strong. I love you and I'm always here for you. Whatever needs to be done is gone be done. That goes without sayin'. You know, people gettin' down in your face. Like you once told me, I was on the outside lookin' in. You know what you know. You know I'm comin' from the heart, man. Don't worry about your family or nothin' like that, 'cause you got a beautiful wife and family, man. All you gotta do is stay strong, run the yard and play ball like I did. You know how I did it. It ain't no thang. We from the west side, baby. You been in jail before, don't buy nothin' and won't nobody sell you nothin'. If a mothafucka' get down wrong then take care of your business, man.

As far as that is concerned, that goes for any of my homeboys that's from Detroit. Ya'll gotta' stick together, 'cause there is safety in numbers, ya' know. The Federal system ain't no joke. That goes for the State system too, but I don't even worry about none of my homeboys there, 'cause they already know how to play it.

What's up Big Joe? That's my man. Joe Griffin. Hey, holler at my man Papa Dupree for me.

Papa stay outta' trouble and come on home. Ain't nothin' happenin' in there. I talked to X. the other day. X. told me that he got a paper route, ha, ha, ha. That boy X. is a mothafucka'! Ain't he Papa? Well, you're up in Brooks. Whenever you get a little closer, I'm gone come and see you, man.

What's up Fat Kevin? You fat bitch. Don't be writin' that mothafuckin' shit to my man Fat Boy. He ain't tryna' hear that shit. Lay down and do that mothafuckin' bit.

I'm on top of the world, Ma. That's my man Cody Jerit. Hey Cody, everythang gone be alright man.

What's up there R.R. I hope when you get out you get yourself together. I don't think you tryna' see me, 'cause I ain't ta' be fucked with. Not on no beefin' tip, 'cause I don't quit. Y.B.I. till the day I die, nigga'.

List of 41 indicted by U.S. jury

The following 41 men and women were named yesterday in federal indictments as members of the narcotics organization Young Boys Inc.:

Sylvester "Seal" Murray, Milton David "Butch" Jones, Velma Bailes, Maurice Bell, Steven Andre Brown, Karen "Kim" Brown.

Eli Carter; Betty Crawford, alias Betty Mallory; Ferrar Crawford; Emanuel Cromer; Ida Mae Chapman; Herbert Daniels; Richard Daniels; Melvin Davenport, also known as Samuel Livingston or "Sammy D."

Andre Diggs; John "Creeper" Doe, Ardie Mae Easterly, John Fullivove; Delos "Pete" Fulwylie, Keith Futtrell; Maurice Gibbs; Karl Gatlin, also known as "Pratt."

Ricky Humphries; Michael "Big Mike" Jenkins, Alonzo Long; Rodney Mason; Lewis McClaine; Denise Murray; Curtis Napier; Timothy Peoples; Raymond Peoples.

George Sanders; Art Sellars; Virdell "Bonnie" Shipp; Tamara Sparks; Paul Smith; Portia Sturdivant, alias Portia Jones; James Thorpe; John Thomas; Kevin Wilson; Darryl Young.

To be Continued...